BON APPÉTIT®

FAVORITES!
CLASSIC RECIPES

VOLUME ONE

BON APPETIT PUBLISHING CORP.
PUBLISHER

LOS ANGELES

INTRODUCTION

"Have you got a great recipe for...?"

Fill in the blank with any old-fashioned favorite you might care to mention—from fried chicken to tomato soup, coleslaw to fudge brownies—and you have what may well be the most popular conversational starter at kitchen tables and over backyard fences nationwide.

We can't stop talking about food. Why should we? Sharing a meal with family or friends is one of life's great pleasures.

And sharing is what *BON APPÉTIT Favorites: Classic Recipes* is all about. It's our chance to share with you well more than one hundred of the most popular versions of time-honored favorites to appear in the pages of *Bon Appétit* over the past decade.

Organized by courses of the meal and by featured ingredients, they include fabulous appetizers and drinks; satisfying soups and salads; main courses both elegant and casual; pastas, pizzas, and sandwiches perfect for informal gatherings; egg and cheese dishes ideal for breakfast or brunch; side dishes to add that something extra to any meal; home-baked breads; and an abundance of enticing desserts.

Throughout the book, we've also included a number of helpful guidelines, tips, and hints to make your daily cooking and special-occasion entertaining easier and more enjoyable than ever.

Together with its companion volume, *New for the '90s,* this book strives to offer you a sampling of the very best of *Bon Appétit.* We hope the recipes give you as much pleasure in your own kitchen as they have in ours for many years.

On the cover: Toffee Cheesecake with Caramel Sauce
Photograph by Brian Leatart

BON APPÉTIT®

Favorites!

Classic Recipes

VOLUME ONE

CONTENTS

continued on next page

Appetizers & Beverages

Fancy something elegant to start a meal? Try a traditional Coeur à la Crème with Caviar, accompanied by iced vodka. How about something more on the casual side? Spicy Cocktail Party Meatballs or a Hot Clam Dip, served with a classic Bloody Mary, will do the trick. Time and time again, the following recipes have started meals and parties with festive style and abundant flavor.

Appetizers

SCHOONER SALAD

4 SERVINGS

1½ pounds ¾-inch-thick firm-fleshed
    white fish, such as sea bass
1 tablespoon lemon juice
1 cup chopped celery
1 cup chopped dill pickle
1 tomato, chopped
½ cup mayonnaise
¼ teaspoon dried dill weed
    Salt and pepper
    Lettuce leaves

Preheat broiler. Broil fish until opaque, about 3 minutes per side. Let cool. Flake fish into pieces with fork. Transfer to bowl. Sprinkle lemon juice over. Add celery, pickle, tomato, mayonnaise and dill and toss. Season with salt and pepper. Cover and refrigerate until chilled. Serve salad on lettuce leaves.

COEUR A LA CREME WITH CAVIAR

This is an elegant and sumptuous first course. Accompany with icy vodka or dry champagne and crisp hot toast.

If the price of caviar seems a bit steep (and it is!), you can serve the *coeur à la crème* more traditionally for dessert with crushed strawberries or raspberries. In that case, beat in 2 tablespoons powdered sugar with cream. Surround with crushed, sweetened strawberries or raspberries.

6 SERVINGS

2 cups cottage cheese
2 cups cream cheese
2 cups whipping cream
    Salt

    Red and black caviar

Beat cheeses together until smooth, using an electric mixer or food processor. Gradually beat in cream, add salt to taste and blend well.

Turn mixture into 6 individual cheesecloth-lined, heart-shaped baskets or molds with perforated bottoms made especially for *coeur à la crème*. Place on rack over a plate and refrigerate overnight to allow whey to drain. (If you have no baskets or molds, let mixture drain in colander lined with cheesecloth and then pack into bowl or heart-shaped cake pan.)

When ready to serve, unmold onto chilled plates. Place a dollop of black caviar on one side and red on the other.

COCKTAIL PARTY MEATBALLS

MAKES 100 SMALL MEATBALLS

2 pounds lean ground beef
¼ cup peeled grated potato
1 egg
1 small onion, grated
    Salt and freshly ground pepper
1 13-ounce bottle chili sauce
5 ounces grape jelly
    Dash of Worcestershire sauce

Combine first 4 ingredients in large bowl and mix well. Season with salt and pepper. Form into small meatballs and set aside.

Blend remaining ingredients in large skillet over medium heat. Add meatballs. Cover and simmer about 30 minutes, stirring occasionally. Transfer meatballs to chafing dish or fondue pot. Skim excess fat from sauce. Pour sauce over meatballs. Serve warm from chafing dish.

Hot Clam Dip

Great for large gatherings.

MAKES 1½ QUARTS

½ cup (1 stick) butter
4 large onions, diced
2 6½-ounce cans minced clams, drained
2 cans white clam sauce
1 can whole baby clams, drained
8 ounces crackers, mashed

½ teaspoon garlic powder
Assorted crudités

Preheat oven to 350°F. Melt butter in large saucepan over medium heat. Add onion and sauté until transparent. Reduce heat to low and add all remaining ingredients except crudités. Cook until heated through, about 8 minutes, stirring frequently. Transfer to baking dish, cover and bake 15 minutes. Remove cover and bake an additional 15 minutes. Serve hot with an assortment of crudités.

Spinach Dip

The spinach can be cooked and chilled in advance, but assemble all ingredients just before serving.

MAKES 3 TO 3½ CUPS

1 cup lowfat cottage cheese
1 cup plain lowfat yogurt
1 10-ounce package frozen, chopped spinach, cooked, cooled and very well drained

1 cup finely chopped green onion
2 tablespoons fresh lime or lemon juice
½ to 1 teaspoon curry powder
Salt and freshly ground pepper

Combine cottage cheese and yogurt in blender and whirl until smooth. Transfer to medium bowl and combine with remaining ingredients.

Salsa Cruda Dip

MAKES ABOUT 2 CUPS

6 to 8 green tomatoes, peeled and quartered, or 1½ cups canned tomatillos, drained
1 medium onion, cut into pieces
½ cup diced canned green chilies
2 jalapeño peppers, seeded and minced, or to taste
1 teaspoon salt
Tortilla chips

Purée tomatoes or tomatillos in processor or blender. Add all remaining ingredients except chips and mix well. Transfer to serving bowl, cover and refrigerate. Serve with tortilla chips.

THREE-CHEESE BALL

MAKES ABOUT 2½ CUPS

1 8-ounce package cream cheese, room temperature
5 ounces cheddar cheese spread, room temperature
10 ounces blue cheese, room temperature
1 small onion, minced
1 garlic clove, minced
2 tablespoons brandy or medium dry sherry
Chopped nuts (optional)
Apples or crackers

Beat cheeses until well mixed and fluffy. Add onion, garlic and liquor and mix well. Chill. Shape into ball, coating with nuts, if desired. Chill again briefly before serving. Serve with slices of unpeeled apple and/or crackers.

Keeps several weeks in refrigerator.

SWEET POTATO RIBBON CHIPS
A sophisticated, do-ahead hors d'oeuvre.

8 SERVINGS

4 medium orange-fleshed sweet potatoes (sometimes known as yams), peeled

Vegetable oil (for deep frying)
Salt

Place potato flat on work surface, holding one end. Using vegetable peeler and starting at center of potato, shave into long, wide ribbons in quick strokes. Turn potato and continue shaving opposite end. Turn potato over and repeat process for each side. Repeat with remaining potatoes.

Heat oil to 375°F in heavy, wide, 4-inch-deep pot. Shake one handful of potatoes into oil; do not crowd. Fry until crisp and slightly golden, stirring occasionally, 30 to 60 seconds. Remove with slotted spoon; drain on paper towels. Season with salt. Repeat with remaining potatoes in batches. (*Can be prepared 6 hours ahead. Cover lightly and store at room temperature.*)

LIPTAUER SPREAD
Serve with thinly sliced dark bread.

MAKES ABOUT 1½ CUPS

1 cup cream cheese
¼ cup (½ stick) unsalted butter
3 tablespoons sour cream
1 tablespoon minced onion
4 anchovy fillets, minced
2 teaspoons drained, chopped capers
1 teaspoon hot paprika or to taste
1 teaspoon caraway seeds
1 teaspoon dry mustard
Salt and white pepper to taste

Combine all ingredients. Beat in electric mixer, blender or food processor with steel knife until fluffy.

QUICK IDEAS FOR HORS D'OEUVRES

Serve crabmeat fingers (the tiny, sweet-meated claws)—fresh, frozen or canned—as a deliciously delicate and not-too-filling appetizer. Arrange the crab fingers around the perimeter of a blue and white platter. In the center place a little bowl of piquant dipping sauce.

Drain a can of artichoke bottoms. Cream together 1 cup fresh ricotta cheese, a few tablespoons of chopped lean prosciutto ham, ¼ cup finely chopped green onion, a dash or two of Worcestershire sauce, and ¼ cup of finely minced cilantro (use Italian parsley if cilantro is not available). Mound the mixture in the artichoke bottoms. Lay a strip of bright red pimiento across the tops. Cut the stuffed artichokes into quarters.

Potted shrimp makes a great appetizer. Have ready eight demitasses or diminutive pôts de crème pots. You'll need two 7½-ounce cans of small shrimp, drained. Place 1 can of shrimp in food processor. Add ¼ pound softened sweet butter, a good dash of Worcestershire sauce, 2 teaspoons lemon juice, 1 teaspoon grated onion, salt and freshly ground pepper. Blend until smooth. Transfer to a bowl. Now add the second can of shrimp, left whole or cut in half, and mix with a wooden spoon until smooth. Pack the mixture into the cups, cover and chill overnight. Serve the cups on saucers, placing a sprig of parsley on top of each cup and a small wedge of lemon on the saucer. Serve with rounds of melba toast.

Pâté and good red wine are ready revivers. A suavely silken chicken liver pâté is quickly made in the food processor. Sauté one pound of chicken livers in a little sweet butter until the livers lose their pink color. Turn into your food processor, add half a small white onion, ½ stick of softened sweet butter, 3 tablespoons Cognac, 1 tablespoon lemon juice, salt and pepper and a miser's pinch of allspice, cloves and thyme. Blend until puréed and smooth. Pack into a lidded earthenware crock and store in the refrigerator. This will keep up to a week.

Pour amontillado sherry in all-purpose wine glasses and surround with inviting nibbles; toasted almonds; pecans; green, black and stuffed olives; a platter of mild cheeses.

Beverages

Banana Daiquiri

ABOUT 6 SERVINGS

2 cups ½-inch ice cubes (or use crushed or shaved)

6 ounces (¾ cup) light rum

4 ounces (½ cup) sweet-and-sour mix

4 ounces (½ cup) half-and-half

2 ounces (¼ cup) Triple Sec or curaçao

2 very ripe medium or large bananas

Orange slices (optional garnish)

Put ice into blender. Add remaining ingredients except orange slices and blend on high or frappé speed about 1½ minutes. Serve in stemmed glasses, garnished if desired.

Wassail Bowl

Though you may find it odd, the appearance of toast slices in the wassail cups was considered a great treat by those in the know in Merry Olde England. In fact, the good cheer and kind wishes that inevitably accompany a few rounds of wassail gave rise to the expression "drinking a toast."

8 SERVINGS

8 small apples, cored

2½ cups firmly packed brown sugar

3 quarts ale or beer

1 fifth sweet sherry or Madeira

4 slices fresh ginger

1½ teaspoons freshly grated nutmeg

1 teaspoon ginger

¼ teaspoon mace

4 whole cloves

4 allspice berries

6 eggs, separated

1 cup brandy, heated

8 slices buttered toast, quartered (optional)

Preheat oven to 400°F. Place apples in baking dish and sprinkle with ½ cup brown sugar. Bake 30 minutes. In large saucepan, heat ale or beer and sherry, remaining brown sugar, and spices tied in a bag. Using large bowl, beat egg yolks until thick. Beat egg whites until stiff peaks form and fold into yolks. Slowly add liquid to eggs by tablespoons until about 1 cup has been added, then add remaining liquid in slow, steady stream, beating well with whisk. Place baked apples in heated punch bowl, add liquid and stir in brandy. Serve at once with buttered toast quarters to float or dip in wassail.

BLOODY MARY

For each serving:

3 ounces tomato juice

1½ ounces vodka

Juice of ½ fresh lemon or lime plus rind

½ teaspoon Worcestershire sauce

Several dashes (approximately ⅛ teaspoon) hot pepper sauce

2 grindings freshly ground pepper

Pinch of celery salt

Pinch of salt

Ice cubes

Celery or cucumber sticks (optional garnish)

Combine all ingredients except ice and garnish in 8- to 10-ounce glass. Stir gently. Add ice and serve garnished or not as you prefer.

STOCKING THE BAR

BASIC BAR

Vodka (2 quarts)	Dry Vermouth (1 fifth)
Scotch (2 quarts)	Sweet Vermouth (1 fifth)
Gin (2 fifths)	Campari (2 fifths)
Bourbon (1 fifth)	Dubonnet (2 fifths)
Blended Whiskey (1 fifth)	White Wine (3 bottles varietal)
Rum (1 fifth)	Mineral Water (2 large bottles)

FULL-SCALE BAR

Vodka (2 quarts domestic; 1 fifth imported)	Dubonnet (1 fifth)
Scotch (2 quarts blended; 1 fifth single malt)	Punt e Mes (1 fifth)
Gin (1 quart domestic; 1 fifth imported)	Dry Vermouth (1 fifth)
Bourbon (1 quart)	Sweet Vermouth (2 fifths)
Tennessee Sour Mash (1 fifth)	Campari (1 fifth)
Blended Whiskey (1 fifth American; 1 fifth Canadian)	White Wine (6 bottles varietal)
	Red Wine (2 bottles fine claret)
Rum (1 fifth Puerto Rican light; 1 fifth Puerto Rican golden; 1 fifth Jamaican dark)	Champagne (1 bottle French; 1 bottle California)
Tequila (1 fifth)	Beer (2 six-packs German or Dutch)
Pernod (1 fifth)	Crème de Cassis (1 small bottle)
Lillet (1 fifth)	Mineral Water (6 bottles)

THE PUNCH BOWL

Classic wine and food combinations carry over into the punch bowl—and with sufficient leeway for improvisation. Champagne and strawberries are compatible and cheerful, as are red wine and spices, brandy and pears. Pink champagne, cold duck and ever-reliable vin rosé make eye-catching additions. Most champagnes, even those labeled dry, are slightly sweet and the inexpensive wines may contain sugar as well. That's why some recipes instruct that punches be "sweetened to taste." For extra aromatics, add an ounce or two of liqueur.

SPECIAL TIPS

Adding fresh lemon—its juice, zest, or both—is wonderfully effective in making a drink really refreshing and appealing. In drinks, as in cooking, the zesty flavor of the lemon blends beautifully with other ingredients and, in fact, magically brings out and enhances the best in their intrinsic flavors.

Guests tend to congregate around the bowl. Help the conversation along by floating something attractive in it. You can make your own block of ice, using any handy mold, even an empty half-gallon milk carton. Add chunks or slices of fruit and water, and freeze. Float oranges sliced into cartwheels; use sliced lemons or limes or both. Orange segments and slices of pear can be frozen and dropped into glasses to serve as additional "ice."

Make your own personal recipe changes only with the greatest of care, remembering that the tastiest blends are a medley of flavors.

Measure all ingredients carefully. Don't imitate free-pouring bartenders who trust a flick of the wrist. The subtle blend of flavors that makes a mixed drink memorable results from a precise combination of ingredients. Many cocktail recipes look deceptively simple, but to throw the ingredients together casually can be disastrous. Use standard measures, whether teaspoons, jiggers, ounces, cups or liters. When you multiply quantities for party drinking, be mathematically accurate.

You don't have to use premium wines or liquors—in fact, you'll be wasting money if you do, because blending overpowers the subtleties that give premium brands their characteristic qualities. But you should like the basic taste of these ingredients because that will remain in the finished blend.

THE PUNCH BOWL

SPECIAL TIPS

If you have trouble igniting brandy, here's a trick: after heating the brandy, take a tablespoon of it and place a sugar cube in the spoon. When the cube has soaked up some liquid, light it, then empty the rest of the tablespoon into the vessel containing the remaining brandy. The sugar will act as a wick, keeping the flame alive.

Unless a recipe advises to the contrary, don't cut fruit until just before serving. Earlier cutting permits the flavor-carrying juices to flow away; oxidation extracts a toll on taste.

Serve the drink in a suitable glass or cup and be sure that it's sparkling clean. Eye appeal being part of the pleasure of drinking, the wrong serving vessel can destroy the effect you seek.

(Imagine serving eggnog in a mug that conceals the liquid's froth or an aromatic wine punch in an eyedropper-size glass that leaves no room for the aroma to develop.) A cold serving vessel will chill hot drinks prematurely, and one containing residues of detergent may affect taste.

Heat ingredients very carefully. Slow heating gives the flavors time to marry, but boiling drives flavor away and leaves an unpleasant "burned" flavor. Boiling also causes the alcohol to evaporate; the result is a punchless punch. Unless a recipe advises to the contrary, heat only until you see wisps of steam arise.

Soups & Salads

Nothing satisfies on a chilly day like homemade soup—be it a robust Corn Chowder or a smooth Quick Pea Soup. And, when the temperature rises, nothing refreshes quite like a salad—whether a main-course Crunchy Chicken Salad or a crisp accompaniment like Early Dutch Coleslaw. These and the other recipes that follow are sure to become year-round standbys in your own kitchen.

Soups

Quick Pea Soup

Ready in 20 minutes.

6 SERVINGS

3 tablespoons butter
1 10-ounce package frozen peas, thawed
1 Boston lettuce head, chopped
4 green onions, chopped
5 cups canned chicken broth

Salt and pepper
Sour cream
6 mint leaves (optional)

Melt butter in heavy large saucepan over low heat. Add peas, lettuce and onions and cook until onions are just soft, stirring occasionally, about 5 minutes. Add broth. Increase heat and bring to boil. Reduce heat and simmer until peas are tender, about 8 minutes.

Purée soup (in batches, if necessary) in blender. Season with salt and pepper. Rewarm in saucepan until heated through. Ladle soup into bowls. Garnish each with dollop of sour cream and mint leaf.

Potato and Onion Soup

6 SERVINGS

3 tablespoons butter
3 tablespoons olive oil
1½ pounds onions, thinly sliced

4 to 4½ cups canned beef broth
2 pounds russet potatoes, peeled, cut into chunks
Salt and pepper
3 tablespoons Parmesan

Melt butter with oil in heavy large skillet over medium-high heat. Add onions and sauté until golden, about 25 minutes.

Meanwhile, bring 4 cups broth to boil in heavy large saucepan. Add potatoes and cook until tender, about 20 minutes. Drain potatoes, reserving broth. Lightly mash potatoes. Combine with reserved broth in same saucepan. Mix in onions. Cook over medium heat until hot, stirring occasionally and thinning with more broth if desired. Season with salt and pepper. Stir in Parmesan.

Potato-Chive Soup

4 SERVINGS

1½ pounds russet potatoes, peeled, cut into 1-inch pieces
4 cups canned chicken broth

1 cup (about) milk
1 tablespoon butter
1 tablespoon chopped fresh chives
⅓ cup sour cream
Salt and pepper
Additional sour cream

Combine potatoes and broth in heavy 2-quart saucepan. Cover and simmer until potatoes are very tender, stirring occasionally, about 45 minutes. Let mixture cool slightly.

Purée potato mixture in batches in blender or processor. Return soup to saucepan. Stir in enough milk to thin to desired consistency. Mix in butter and chives. Bring to simmer. Remove from heat and mix in ⅓ cup sour cream. Season with salt and pepper. Serve, passing additional sour cream separately.

MUSHROOM AND BARLEY SOUP

8 SERVINGS

1 pound mushrooms
¼ cup (½ stick) butter
1 onion, chopped
1 leek (white and pale green parts only), chopped
8 cups canned chicken broth
1 pound white potatoes (about 2 large), peeled, diced
1 carrot, peeled, chopped
½ cup pearl barley
3 bay leaves
Salt and pepper

Separate mushroom stems from caps. Slice caps and set aside. Chop stems. Melt butter in heavy large saucepan over medium-high heat. Add mushroom stems, onion and leek and sauté until tender, about 8 minutes. Mix in chicken broth, potatoes, carrot, barley and bay leaves. Cover mixture and simmer 30 minutes. Uncover soup, add mushroom caps and continue simmering until vegetables are very tender, about 25 minutes. Season with salt and pepper and serve.

CLASSIC BEET BORSCHT

12 SERVINGS

3 tablespoons butter
3 garlic cloves, minced
1 cup chopped onion
6 cups beef stock or canned low-salt broth
6 cups chicken stock or canned low-salt broth
1 tablespoon minced fresh dill or 1 teaspoon dried dill weed
2 large bunches fresh beets (about 2¼ pounds total), peeled, chopped
1 cup chopped celery
1 cup chopped peeled carrots

Salt and pepper
3 tablespoons (or more) red wine vinegar
5 teaspoons (or more) sugar
Sour cream
Fresh dill sprigs (garnish)

Melt butter in heavy large saucepan over

medium heat. Add garlic and sauté 30 seconds. Add onion and cook until translucent, stirring occasionally, about 8 minutes. Add both stocks and minced dill and bring to boil. Add beets, celery and carrots and cook until vegetables are tender, stirring occasionally, about 25 minutes. *(Can be prepared 1 day ahead. Cover and chill. Bring soup to simmer before continuing.)*

Season soup with salt and pepper. Add 3 tablespoons vinegar and 5 teaspoons sugar. Taste, adding more vinegar and/or sugar to balance flavors, if desired. Ladle into bowls. Top with dollop of sour cream. Garnish with dill.

Corn Chowder

2 SERVINGS

1 17-ounce can creamed corn
2 cups milk (do not use lowfat or nonfat)
1½ cups frozen diced hash brown potatoes (about 6 ounces)
1 green onion, chopped
3 pieces bacon, cooked, crumbled
Salt and pepper

Combine first 5 ingredients in heavy medium saucepan. Simmer over medium heat until soup is slightly thickened, stirring occasionally. Season with salt and pepper and serve.

Vegetable-Sausage Soup

4 TO 6 SERVINGS

1 pound hot or sweet Italian sausage, casings removed
1 large onion, chopped
2 carrots, sliced
1 cup sliced mushrooms
⅓ cup chopped fresh parsley
2 garlic cloves, minced
3 cups canned beef broth
1 15½-ounce can chickpeas (garbanzo beans), drained
2 cups water
1 cup beer
1 teaspoon dried basil, crumbled
½ teaspoon ground or rubbed dried sage
Salt and pepper
Additional chopped fresh parsley

Cook sausage in medium Dutch oven over medium-high heat until brown, breaking up with fork, about 7 minutes. Add onion, carrots, mushrooms, ⅓ cup parsley and garlic and cook until onion is translucent, stirring frequently, about 5 minutes. Mix in next 6 ingredients. Simmer 15 minutes. Season with salt and pepper. Ladle soup into bowls. Sprinkle with additional chopped parsley.

TOMATO AND SPINACH SOUP

4 SERVINGS

2 28-ounce cans tomatoes
¼ cup (½ stick) butter
1 onion, finely chopped
1 teaspoon sugar
¼ teaspoon dried oregano, crumbled
½ cup whipping cream
1 10-ounce package frozen chopped
   spinach, thawed, well drained
¼ cup chopped fresh basil or
   1 tablespoon dried, crumbled
   Salt and pepper
½ cup (about) milk (optional)
½ cup grated Parmesan

Purée canned tomatoes with juices in processor or blender until smooth. Melt butter in heavy large saucepan over medium-low heat. Add onion and sauté until very tender, about 5 minutes. Stir in tomatoes, sugar and oregano. Simmer 10 minutes. Mix in cream, spinach and basil and simmer 3 minutes longer. Season to taste with salt and pepper. Thin soup with milk if desired. Ladle soup into bowls; pass Parmesan separately.

CREAM OF SPINACH SOUP

This soup can also be served chilled.

2 TO 4 SERVINGS

1 10-ounce package frozen spinach
   soufflé, thawed
1 10½-ounce can cream of potato
   soup
1½ cups milk
¼ cup sour cream
1 green onion, sliced
1 teaspoon fresh lemon juice
   Pinch of dried thyme
   Pepper

Place all ingredients in blender and blend until smooth. Transfer to heavy large saucepan. Bring soup to boil over medium-high heat, stirring frequently. Ladle into bowls and serve.

CHILLED TOMATO AND ORANGE SOUP

8 SERVINGS

6 medium oranges

3 tablespoons unsalted butter
1½ cups thinly sliced yellow onions
½ cup thinly sliced fennel bulb
2½ pounds plum tomatoes, quartered
½ cup dry white wine
1 tablespoon grated orange peel
1 bay leaf
1 teaspoon salt
3½ cups chicken stock or canned
   low-salt broth

½ cup sour cream or plain yogurt
   Fresh basil sprigs (garnish)

Using small sharp knife, cut off peel and white pith from oranges. Working over bowl to catch juice, cut between membranes to release segments.

   Melt butter in heavy large saucepan over low heat. Add sliced onions and fennel and sauté 10 minutes. Add half of oranges with their juices and half of tomatoes and simmer 10 minutes, stirring occasionally. Add dry white wine, grated orange peel, bay leaf and salt. Mix in remaining oranges with their juices, remaining tomatoes and chicken stock. Bring to boil. Reduce heat to medium and cook soup 10 minutes, stirring occasionally. Discard bay leaf.

Purée soup in blender or processor in batches. Cover and chill soup until cold *(Can be prepared 2 days ahead.)*

Ladle soup into bowls. Top with dollop of sour cream or yogurt. Garnish with fresh basil sprigs and serve.

SHRIMP AND CORN CHOWDER

6 TO 8 SERVINGS

1 pound russet potatoes, peeled and chopped
2 onions, chopped
1 large red bell pepper, seeded and chopped
4 cups water
1 17-ounce can creamed corn
1 17-ounce can whole-kernel corn, drained
1 cup whipping cream
1 cup milk
 Salt and pepper
½ pound uncooked medium shrimp, peeled and deveined
 Chopped fresh chives (garnish)

Place first 3 ingredients in heavy large Dutch oven. Pour water over. Bring to boil. Reduce heat and simmer until potatoes are tender, about 20 minutes. Stir in both cans of corn, cream and milk. Season with salt and pepper. Simmer 20 minutes. Add shrimp and cook until opaque, about 8 minutes. Garnish soup with chives.

A PERFECT COLD SOUP

For a perfect cold soup to start a summer brunch, combine 3 cups chopped cantaloupe and 3 cups chopped honeydew. Purée half of mixture and finely chop the other half. Blend 2 cups fresh orange juice and about 3 tablespoons honey into the puréed melon, then add 2 cups brut Champagne and the remaining finely chopped melon. Serve the soup well chilled. For added elegance serve it in crystal or glass stemware.

Salads

ITALIAN CHOPPED SALAD

1 large head romaine lettuce, finely chopped
4 large plum tomatoes, seeded, finely chopped
1 green bell pepper, finely chopped
4 ounces Italian dry salami, finely chopped
1 cup drained canned chickpeas (garbanzo beans)
4½ ounces mozzarella, diced
½ cup pitted black olives, finely chopped
½ cup pimiento-stuffed green olives, finely chopped
¾ cup olive oil
2 tablespoons red wine vinegar
1½ tablespoons minced fresh basil or 1 teaspoon dried, crumbled
1 tablespoon Dijon mustard
2 teaspoons fresh lemon juice
Pinch of sugar
Salt and pepper

Combine first 8 ingredients in large bowl. Blend oil with next 5 ingredients in small bowl. Season with salt and pepper. Pour over salad and toss thoroughly.

CRUNCHY CHICKEN SALAD

4 SERVINGS

3 cups coarsely chopped cooked chicken (about 1 pound)
1 cup chopped celery
1 cup toasted slivered almonds
½ cup mayonnaise
2 tablespoons lemon juice
2 tablespoons chopped fresh parsley
Salt and pepper

Combine first 6 ingredients in large bowl. Season with salt and pepper. Toss to blend thoroughly.

BACON AND BLUE CHEESE SALAD WITH CAESAR DRESSING

A delicious blend of classic flavors.

4 SERVINGS

1 large romaine lettuce head, torn into bite-size pieces
6 bacon slices, cooked, crumbled
½ cup crumbled blue cheese (about 2 ounces)
Easy Caesar Dressing (see recipe)
1 cup Garlic Croutons (see recipe)

Place first 3 ingredients in large bowl. Add enough dressing to season to taste and toss well. Garnish salad with croutons and serve.

EASY CAESAR DRESSING

MAKES ABOUT 1 CUP

½ cup freshly grated Parmesan (about 2 ounces)
¼ cup plus 2 tablespoons olive oil

¼ cup plus 2 tablespoons vegetable
   oil
¼ cup fresh lemon juice
2 garlic cloves
1 teaspoon Worcestershire sauce

Combine all ingredients in blender or
processor. Blend until smooth. Season to
taste with salt and pepper. *(Can be prepared 2 days ahead. Cover and refrigerate.)*

GARLIC CROUTONS

MAKES ABOUT 3 CUPS

2 tablespoons (¼ stick) butter
¼ cup olive oil
2 large garlic cloves, pressed
4 French bread slices, cut into
   ¾-inch cubes
Salt and pepper

Preheat oven to 350°F. Melt 2 tablespoons
butter with olive oil and garlic in small
saucepan. Place bread cubes on baking
sheet. Pour butter mixture over and toss

well. Bake until bread cubes are golden
brown and crisp, about 20 minutes.
Season with salt and pepper. Cool completely. *(Croutons can be prepared 1 day
ahead. Store at room temperature in airtight container.)*

EARLY DUTCH COLESLAW

*Can be prepared three days ahead. Sur-
round with cabbage leaves for attractive
serving. The dressing for this delicious
coleslaw dates back to the first Dutch
settlers in America.*

12 SERVINGS

DRESSING

3 eggs
¾ cup cider vinegar
1½ tablespoons dry mustard
2 teaspoons sugar (optional)
1 teaspoon salt
½ teaspoon celery seed
⅛ teaspoon freshly ground pepper

3 tablespoons butter or bacon fat
2 tablespoons all purpose flour
1 cup milk
   Salt and pepper

COLESLAW

7 cups shredded green cabbage
¾ cup minced onion
½ cup chopped pimiento
½ cup sour cream
¼ cup minced celery
¼ cup minced green pepper
3 tablespoons minced fresh parsley
   Salt and freshly ground pepper

FOR DRESSING: Combine eggs, vinegar,
mustard, sugar, salt, celery seed and
pepper in medium mixing bowl and
beat until smooth. Set aside.

Melt butter in heavy nonaluminum
1½-quart saucepan over medium heat. Stir
in flour and cook, whisking constantly,
about 3 minutes, reducing heat if necessary so flour does not brown. Pour in
milk and continue whisking until sauce
begins to simmer. Cook, whisking con-

stantly, about 5 minutes. Reduce heat to just below simmer, stir in egg mixture and cook until sauce thickens; do not boil, or eggs will curdle. Remove from heat and let cool. Season to taste. Transfer to container, cover and refrigerate up to 5 days.

FOR COLESLAW: Combine cabbage, onion, pimiento, sour cream, celery, green pepper and parsley in large mixing bowl and toss lightly. Add dressing and toss again. Season with salt and pepper to taste. Cover and refrigerate 1 to 3 days.

GREEK SALAD

8 SERVINGS

½ head romaine lettuce, torn into pieces
½ head iceberg lettuce, torn into pieces
1 cucumber, peeled, sliced
1 bell pepper, sliced
½ red onion, thinly sliced
2 celery stalks, chopped
1 large tomato, diced
½ cup sliced black olives
8 ounces feta cheese, crumbled
⅔ cup purchased olive oil and vinegar dressing
½ teaspoon dried oregano, crumbled
½ teaspoon dried dill weed
½ teaspoon pepper

Combine first 8 ingredients in large salad bowl. Sprinkle with feta. Whisk dressing, herbs and pepper in bowl to blend. Pour over salad. Toss well.

CORN AND BELL PEPPER SALAD

2 SERVINGS; CAN BE DOUBLED OR TRIPLED

1 10-ounce package frozen whole-kernel corn, cooked according to package directions, drained
½ red bell pepper, diced
½ green bell pepper, diced
2 green onions, chopped
2 tablespoons (generous) chopped fresh cilantro
2 tablespoons olive oil
2 teaspoons fresh lime juice
¼ teaspoon ground cumin
Salt and freshly ground pepper
Red lettuce leaves
Fresh cilantro sprigs

Mix first 8 ingredients in medium bowl. Season with salt and pepper. Place red lettuce leaves on plates. Spoon salad onto lettuce. Top with fresh cilantro sprigs and serve.

GUILT-FREE SOUR CREAM

LAND O'LAKES HAS CREATED A LIGHT sour cream with two-thirds less fat and one-third fewer calories than its rich cousin. The "light" comes from skim milk, which replaces the full-fat cream used in the original. Available in supermarkets nationwide. For a free recipe booklet, call 800-782-9602.

SPINACH, BACON AND APPLE SALAD

6 SERVINGS

¼ cup olive oil
3 tablespoons wine vinegar
1 teaspoon sugar
½ teaspoon prepared mustard
  Salt and freshly ground pepper
5 slices bacon
⅓ cup sliced almonds
1 pound fresh spinach (stems discarded), torn into bite-size pieces
1 unpeeled red apple, cored and coarsely chopped
3 green onions, thinly sliced

Combine first 4 ingredients with salt and pepper in jar with tight-fitting lid and shake well. Refrigerate until ready to use.

Cook bacon in large skillet over medium-high heat until browned and crisp. Drain well on paper towels. Crumble and set aside. Discard all but 1 tablespoon fat from skillet. Add almonds to skillet and shake pan over medium-high heat until nuts are lightly toasted. Remove from heat. Combine spinach with bacon, apple, onion and almonds and toss lightly. Shake dressing, pour over salad and toss again.

TUNA AND WHITE BEAN SALAD

The Mediterranean heritage of this lively salad accounts for both its robustness and piquancy. Serve it with hot Italian bread or rolls with fresh sweet butter and sip Chablis or Chardonnay. For dessert: fruit ice, sorbet or sherbet and butter cookies.

4 TO 6 SERVINGS

2 cups white beans
  Salt

2 red or green peppers
½ cup chopped red onion
¼ cup chopped parsley
3 tablespoons olive oil
1 tablespoon wine vinegar
  Salt and pepper
  Lettuce
2 7-ounce cans tuna (Italian variety packed in olive oil, if possible)
  Lemon slices and oil-cured black olives (garnish)

In medium saucepan, boil beans 2 minutes in water to cover. Remove from heat and let stand, tightly covered, 1 hour. Add more water to cover and salt to taste and simmer beans until tender, 20 to 30 minutes. Drain and set aside.

Preheat broiler when beans are almost cooked. Place peppers on rack or in pan and broil until skin blackens and can be removed. Cut into strips. Combine pepper strips, onion and parsley with warm beans. Toss with olive oil, vinegar, salt and pepper. Taste and adjust seasoning, if necessary.

Spoon salad onto four or six lettuce-lined plates. Separate tuna into chunks and arrange around beans, alternating with lemon slices and olives. Serve this salad at room temperature.

Avocado and Shrimp Salad

4 SERVINGS

3 tablespoons olive oil
2 tablespoons white wine vinegar (preferably French)
1 teaspoon Dijon mustard
1 pound fresh shrimp, cooked, shelled, deveined and cubed
1 cup mayonnaise
2 tablespoons chili sauce
1 large garlic clove, crushed
  Hot pepper sauce
  Salt and freshly ground pepper
1 ripe large avocado
  Juice of ½ lemon
2 tablespoons finely minced fresh dill
2 tablespoons finely minced fresh chives
  Dill sprigs, lemon wedges and avocado slices (garnish)

Whisk together first 3 ingredients until well blended. Add to shrimp, toss thoroughly, cover and marinate.

Meanwhile, whisk mayonnaise, chili sauce, garlic, hot pepper sauce, salt and pepper until smooth. Set aside.

Peel, pit and cube avocado. Sprinkle with lemon juice.

Drain shrimp. Add cubed avocado, dill and chives and toss lightly. Fold in enough mayonnaise mixture to coat lightly. Taste and adjust seasoning. Cover and chill until ready to serve.

Divide salad among chilled plates and garnish with dill sprigs, lemon wedges and avocado slices.

Super Potato Salad

6 SERVINGS

3½ pounds (about 6 large) russet potatoes, scrubbed
6 hard-boiled eggs, sliced
8 radishes, chopped
4 green onions, sliced
½ cup chopped bread and butter pickles
5 bacon slices, fried, crumbled
½ cup toasted sliced almonds
½ green bell pepper, diced

½ cup buttermilk
½ cup sour cream
½ cup mayonnaise
½ 1-ounce envelope ranch salad dressing mix
1 tablespoon Dijon mustard
½ teaspoon dried dill weed
  Salt and pepper
  Chopped fresh parsley (garnish)

Place russet potatoes in large pot. Add water to cover. Boil until potatoes are tender but not mushy, about 35 minutes. Cool potatoes completely. Peel potatoes and dice. Place in large bowl. Add next 7 ingredients.

Mix buttermilk, sour cream, mayonnaise, dressing mix, mustard and dill weed in small bowl. Pour over potato mixture and toss well. Season with salt and pepper. Garnish with parsley.

DRESSING IDEAS

- To dress a salad of seasonal greens, try a vinaigrette made with fragrantly fruity, ruby-red raspberry vinegar combined with a light French olive oil. The raspberry taste, with its delicate flavor and hint of sweetness, offers an unusual foil for the greens.

- With crinkly forest-green spinach leaves and sliced raw mushrooms, combine a full-bodied red wine vinegar, with salad oil and a miser's touch of Dijon mustard.

- Serve an attractive mélange of briefly cooked snow pea pods, raw turnips or black winter radishes and mushrooms dressed with a light vinaigrette. Cook fresh or frozen Chinese pea pods in boiling water 2 minutes; drain and cut into julienne strips. Peel white turnips (or tart, firm winter radishes), slice thinly, then stack the slices and cut into julienne strips. Wipe fresh white mushrooms with damp towel, cut off stems and slice caps as thinly as possible. Sprinkle the mushrooms with a little lemon juice to keep them white. Combine vegetables in a large bowl and toss very gently with light oil, vinegar, garlic powder, salt and fresh pepper.

- With tart, crunchy sliced endive bejeweled with bright green shards of scallion use a dressing of champagne vinegar and light French olive oil, a flick of tarragon leaves and pepper.

- For an unusual salad and crunch, color and zest, slice red radishes into paper-thin rounds, sprinkle with rounds of sliced green onion and drizzle with lemon juice. Serve on chilled plates with a lemon wedge.

- For barely cooked florets of broccoli or cauliflower use a dressing of sherry wine vinegar blended with a light oil and a sprinkling of chervil.

- Dress a salad of cubed fresh apples, pineapple and pears with a vinaigrette made of raspberry vinegar, salad oil and garnish with slivered almonds.

Main Courses

So many main-course dishes remain dear to our hearts. From Steak au Poivre to Osso Buco, Minty Lamb Chops to Sweet and Sour Spareribs, Roast Chicken with Rosemary Butter to Baked Salmon with Champagne and Dill Mayonnaise, the recipes on the following pages—organized into separate sections on beef, veal, lamb, pork, poultry, and fish—promise night after night of memorable dining.

Beef

BASIC PAN-BROILED STEAK

Any tender cut may be used for this easy method. The crusty bits remaining in the skillet may be turned into excellent sauces.

1 TO 4 SERVINGS

2 tablespoons clarified butter or beef fat, or more
1 to 4 steaks, cut at least 1¼ inches thick
Salt and freshly ground pepper

Heat butter over medium-high heat in heavy skillet large enough to hold steaks without touching. Add meat and sear well on both sides, turning with tongs; *do not pierce with fork.* Reduce heat to medium and continue cooking, turning often, to desired degree of doneness. Sprinkle with salt and pepper and serve.

BROCCOLI BEEF

4 SERVINGS

1 pound fresh broccoli, trimmed and peeled
1 tablespoon oil
2 garlic cloves, minced
½ pound lean beef, thinly sliced
½ cup frozen whole pearl onions, thawed and drained
¼ cup diced pimiento
Chow Sauce*

Chow mein noodles or freshly steamed rice

Cook broccoli in boiling water until crisp-tender, about 10 minutes. Drain. Cut off florets; slice broccoli stems diagonally.

Heat wok or skillet over high heat. Add oil and swirl to coat. Add half of garlic and stir-fry briefly; do not burn. Blend in beef and broccoli stems and stir-fry about 2 minutes. Add florets, onions, pimiento, Chow Sauce and garlic.

Cover and cook until vegetables are crisp-tender, about 2 minutes. Serve over noodles or freshly steamed rice.

*CHOW SAUCE

2 tablespoons oyster sauce
2 tablespoons Chinese rice wine
1 tablespoon soy sauce
1 teaspoon cornstarch
½ teaspoon salt

Mix all ingredients in small bowl.

BASIC OVEN-BROILED STEAK

4 SERVINGS

4 tender steaks, cut at least 1½ inches thick
Salt and freshly ground pepper

Set rack 4 inches from heat source and preheat broiler. Place steak on rack set over broiler pan and broil until browned, about 3 minutes per side. Turn oven to 375°F and continue cooking steaks, turning often, until desired degree of doneness is reached. Sprinkle with salt and pepper to taste and serve.

Steak au Poivre

2 SERVINGS

2 tablespoons black peppercorns
2 top loin, rib, T-bone or porterhouse
  steaks, cut at least 1¼ inches thick

2 tablespoons Cognac
2 tablespoons dry red wine
¼ cup beef stock
2 tablespoons whipping cream

Spread peppercorns on board and crush lightly with rolling pin. Press into steaks and pan-broil according to basic recipe. Remove from skillet; keep warm.

Pour off all but 1 tablespoon drippings from pan. Add Cognac and wine, bring to boil over high heat and boil 2 minutes, stirring constantly. Add stock and boil 2 minutes longer, scraping brown bits from pan. Blend in cream and cook just until heated through. Pour over steaks and serve immediately.

Where's the Beef Label?

DESPITE RECENT LABELING REFORMS, it is not mandatory for food companies to list nutrition information on packages of fresh meat and poultry. As a result, the U.S. Department of Agriculture has been under fire from consumer groups who want more from the labels. In response, the agency has proposed a set of voluntary guidelines. Among them is a label that would identify how much sodium, saturated fat and cholesterol are present, as well as how many calories from fat. While the USDA has until 1993 to finalize the guidelines, producers may respond sooner.

Marinated Chuck Steak with Beer and Onions

8 SERVINGS

1 8- to 9-pound chuck steak,
  boned, rolled and tied
2 pounds onions, thinly sliced
2 cups dark beer or ale
½ cup oil
¼ cup cider vinegar
2 large garlic cloves, minced
3 bay leaves
1 tablespoon dry mustard
1¼ teaspoons basil
1 teaspoon freshly ground pepper
1 teaspoon thyme
½ teaspoon oregano
½ teaspoon marjoram

Place steak in large bowl. Combine all remaining ingredients and pour over meat. Cover and refrigerate 2 days, turning meat often.

Preheat oven to 425°F. Drain meat, reserving marinade, and place in Dutch oven or deep roasting pan. Remove onions from marinade with slotted spoon and spread around meat. Place in oven and brown meat well on all sides.

Reduce heat to 350°F and cook 2 to 3 hours, or until meat thermometer indicates desired doneness, basting generously with marinade every 20 minutes. When all marinade has been used, continue to baste with pan juices.

Remove meat from pan and let stand 10 minutes before carving. Skim excess fat from pan, taste and adjust seasonings, if necessary. (Juices may also be reduced over high heat to intensify flavor.) Slice meat, ladle some sauce over and pass remainder separately.

BASIC BARBECUED STEAK

4 SERVINGS

4 tender steaks, cut 1½ to 2 inches thick
Salt and freshly ground pepper

Preheat gas or electric barbecue or prepare briquettes. (If grill has adjustable rack, coals should be white-hot; if non-adjustable, allow coals to burn down a bit more.) Set rack about 2 inches from coals and sear steaks on both sides, about 3 minutes per side for rare meat. Raise rack to 4 inches above coals and continue to cook, turning frequently, until desired degree of doneness is reached.

CALF'S LIVER WITH BACON AND GARLIC

This easy recipe adds a nice hit of sautéed garlic to a classic dish. You can vary the amount of garlic to suit your own taste.

4 SERVINGS

3 bacon slices
4 calf's liver slices (4 ounces each)
  Salt and pepper
  All purpose flour
1 tablespoon butter
8 garlic cloves, thinly sliced
  Chopped fresh parsley

Cook bacon in heavy large skillet over medium heat until crisp. Transfer bacon to paper towel to drain. Crumble bacon. Discard all but 1 tablespoon drippings from skillet. Season liver with salt and pepper. Dredge in flour, shake off excess. Melt butter in same skillet over high heat. Add liver and cook to desired doneness, about 1 minute per side for medium. Transfer liver to plates. Add garlic to skillet and cook until golden, stirring constantly, about 2 minutes. Spoon garlic over liver. Sprinkle with crumbled bacon and parsley and serve.

Meat Loaf Plus

The "plus" in this delicious dish? Chopped green olives, savory onion soup mix and a dash of red wine.

4 SERVINGS

1 pound plus 2 ounces ground beef
1 cup herbed seasoned stuffing
2 eggs, beaten to blend
½ cup dry red wine
10 pimiento-stuffed olives, chopped
3 tablespoons minced fresh parsley
1 envelope onion soup mix
2 garlic cloves, minced
  Salt and pepper

Preheat oven to 350°F. Combine all ingredients in large bowl. Mix thoroughly. Transfer mixture to greased 8½x4½-inch loaf pan. Bake until meat loaf shrinks from sides of pan and top is brown, about 1 hour. Turn out onto platter and serve.

Beef, Mushroom and Broccoli Stir-Fry

2 SERVINGS; CAN BE DOUBLED

½ pound flank steak
1½ tablespoons water
1 tablespoon cornstarch
1 tablespoon soy sauce
1 tablespoon vegetable oil

SAUCE

3 tablespoons canned chicken broth
2 tablespoons dry white wine
1½ tablespoons cornstarch
1 tablespoon soy sauce
1 tablespoon oyster sauce
2 teaspoons Oriental sesame oil
¼ teaspoon sugar

2 tablespoons vegetable oil
3 quarter-size slices peeled fresh
  ginger, minced (about 2 teaspoons)
1 pound broccoli, cut into florets
½ cup canned chicken broth
8 ounces mushrooms, sliced
  Freshly cooked rice

Cut beef with grain into 2-inch-wide pieces, then slice thinly across grain. Combine with next 4 ingredients in medium bowl and stir to coat. Refrigerate at least 30 minutes.

FOR SAUCE: Combine first 7 ingredients in small bowl, stirring to dissolve cornstarch completely.

Heat 1 tablespoon vegetable oil in wok or heavy large skillet over high heat. Add beef with marinade and stir-fry until no longer pink, about 1½ minutes. Transfer to platter. Add remaining 1 tablespoon vegetable oil to wok and heat over high heat. Add ginger and stir until aromatic, about 30 seconds. Add broccoli and stir-fry until dark green, about 1 minute. Add ½ cup broth. Cover, reduce heat and simmer 2 minutes. Add mushrooms, cover and cook until broccoli is just crisp-tender, about 2 minutes. Return beef to wok. Stir sauce, add to wok and stir until sauce thickens, about 30 seconds. Transfer mixture to platter. Serve immediately with freshly cooked rice.

STEAK DIANE

Less tender cuts may also be used if not cooked beyond medium-rare.

2 SERVINGS

2 butterflied tournedos, top loin or rib eye steaks, pan-broiled (see recipe) in clarified butter and kept warm
3 tablespoons minced shallot
2 tablespoons minced parsley
2 tablespoons dry sherry
1 tablespoon Cognac
2 teaspoons steak sauce
1 teaspoon Worcestershire sauce
1 teaspoon Dijon mustard
1 tablespoon minced chives

Combine all ingredients except chives in skillet in which steaks were cooked and boil 3 minutes, scraping brown bits from pan. Taste and adjust seasonings if desired. Stir in chives and pour sauce over steaks. Serve immediately.

BEEF TACOS WITH CHILI TACO SAUCE

If running short on time, substitute purchased crisp taco shells for the freshly made ones. Guests can add their own cheese, lettuce, onion and tomatoes. Offer the remaining Chili Taco Sauce and the Spicy Fresh Salsa alongside.

MAKES 48 TACOS

MEAT FILLING

3 tablespoons olive oil
2 onions, coarsely chopped
3 pounds ground beef (do not use lean)
2 teaspoons minced jalapeño chilies with seeds
2 teaspoons chili powder
1 teaspoon dried oregano, crumbled
2 garlic cloves, minced
1 cup Chili Taco Sauce (see recipe)

TACO SHELLS

Lard or vegetable oil (for deep frying)

48 8-inch-diameter flour tortillas or 6-inch-diameter corn tortillas

Grated Monterey Jack cheese
Grated cheddar cheese
Shredded lettuce
Chopped red onions
Chopped tomatoes
Chili Taco Sauce (see recipe)
Spicy Fresh Salsa (see recipe)

FOR FILLING: Heat oil in heavy large deep skillet over medium heat. Add onions and sauté until soft, about 5 minutes. Add beef, jalapeños, chili powder, oregano and garlic and cook until beef is brown, breaking up with fork, about 15 minutes. Mix in Chili Taco Sauce and bring to simmer. *(Can be prepared 1 day ahead. Cover and chill. Bring to simmer before serving.)*

FOR SHELLS: Heat lard in heavy large saucepan to 375°F to 400°F. Fold tortilla in half. Grasp with tongs and lower into oil. Cook until deep golden brown and crisp, about 3 minutes. Transfer to paper towels and drain. Repeat with remaining tortillas. *(Can be prepared 4 hours ahead. Store airtight.)*

Fill each taco shell with 3 to 4 tablespoons meat filling. Arrange on serving platter. Serve with bowls of grated cheeses, shredded lettuce, onions, tomatoes, taco sauce and salsa.

CHILI TACO SAUCE

MAKES ABOUT 4 CUPS

2 12-ounce jars chili sauce
2 small red onions, finely chopped
½ cup fresh lemon juice
⅓ cup water
2 tablespoons red wine vinegar
1 tablespoon golden brown sugar
1 bay leaf
2 garlic cloves, minced
1 teaspoon hot pepper sauce (such as Tabasco)
1 teaspoon dry mustard
1 teaspoon salt

Combine all ingredients in heavy large saucepan. Bring to boil, stirring occasionally. Reduce heat to low and simmer until thickened slightly, stirring occasionally, about 30 minutes. Cover and refrigerate until well chilled. *(Can be prepared 2 days ahead.)*

SPICY FRESH SALSA

A chunky and highly seasoned salsa, especially good on tacos or with chips.

MAKES ABOUT 4 CUPS

6 large tomatoes
1 onion, chopped
1 cup chopped fresh cilantro
2 fresh Anaheim chilies,* seeded, diced
4 serrano chilies, minced
2 tablespoons red wine vinegar
2 tablespoons olive oil
2 garlic cloves, minced
Salt

Bring large pot of water to boil. Add tomatoes and blanch 30 seconds. Transfer to bowl of cold water using slotted spoon and cool. Drain. Peel off skins using small sharp knife. Seed and chop tomatoes. Transfer to large bowl. Mix in onion, cilantro, Anaheim chilies, serrano chilies, vinegar, oil and garlic. Season with salt. Refrigerate until cold, at least 1 and up to 4 hours.

*Also known as California chilies. Available at Latin American markets and specialty foods stores.

Moussaka (Greek Eggplant-Meat Casserole)

Casserole can be refrigerated or frozen before custard is added. Bring to room temperature before baking.

6 TO 8 SERVINGS

3 or 4 eggplants, peeled and cut into slices ⅜ inch thick
Salted water
Flour

½ cup (about) peanut oil

2 tablespoons olive oil
1 large onion, diced (1 cup)
2 tomatoes, peeled and diced or 2 cups canned plum tomatoes, drained
1½ pounds lean ground beef
1 teaspoon salt
Freshly ground pepper

CUSTARD TOPPING

¼ cup (½ stick) butter
5 tablespoons flour
½ cup whipping cream
1 cup water
½ teaspoon salt
Freshly ground pepper
Dash of nutmeg

1 cup (about) freshly grated Parmesan cheese

2 eggs
2 teaspoons fresh lemon juice

Soak eggplant slices in salted water 20 minutes. Drain, then blot on paper towels. Coat with flour.

Preheat oven to 450°F. Grease 8x15-inch casserole and cover rimmed baking sheet with heavy-duty foil. Coat foil with about ½ cup peanut oil. Add eggplant, turning to coat well. Bake about 20 minutes. Turn off oven and let eggplant stand another 30 minutes.

Heat olive oil in large skillet. Add onion and sauté 1 minute. Add tomatoes and cook another minute. Add beef and cook through. Season to taste with salt and pepper. Drain meat and pour drippings over eggplant slices. Let meat cool while making custard.

Melt butter in medium skillet. Stir in flour and cook 1 minute. Add cream, water, salt, pepper and nutmeg and cook until very thick, about 10 to 12 minutes, stirring frequently. Remove from heat, cover and set aside.

Preheat oven to 350°F. Layer eggplant and meat mixture to within 1 inch of top of casserole, sprinkling each layer with cheese. Bake 15 minutes.

Beat eggs and whisk into cooled cream sauce. Add lemon juice. Taste and adjust seasoning. Spoon over casserole. Continue baking on lowest shelf of oven until hot, browned and puffed, about 35 minutes. Cut into squares.

BASIC IDEAS FOR GROUND BEEF

■ Combine 2 pounds lean ground beef with 1 egg, ½ cup soy sauce and ¼ cup each chopped red pepper, onion and pine nuts. Generously season mixture with herb seasoning blend and garlic powder. Form it into patties and broil, barbecue or pan-fry to desired doneness.

■ In addition to hamburgers, ground beef can be used for a myriad of other simple suppers. And meat loaf is probably one of the easiest! Just mix together 1½ pounds lean ground beef, 1 8-ounce can tomato sauce with mushrooms, 1 lightly beaten egg and 1 3-ounce can fried onion rings, crumbled coarsely, in a large bowl. Pack the entire mixture in a 9x5-inch loaf pan and bake 45 to 50 minutes.

■ Add a fancy flair to 6 plain, uncooked meat patties (about ¼ to ¾ inch thick) seasoned with garlic powder, salt and pepper by topping each with about ½ cup wild rice, prepared according to package directions. Roll the patties up, with the rice inside, and secure them with toothpicks. Place them seam side down in an oiled baking dish and cover with a sauce made from a 10½-ounce can cream of mushroom soup and 2 tablespoons catsup. Bake for 1 hour in a 350° oven.

■ A special trick with hamburgers is to lightly shape each patty around a small ice cube to keep the meat moist.

■ Making chili is ridiculously easy by adding 2 15½-ounce cans kidney beans, drained, 2 10½-ounce cans tomato soup and 1½ soup cans water to 1 pound lean ground beef that has been browned in olive oil and drained. Bring entire mixture to a boil, then reduce heat to medium. Add 2 large onions, minced, and cover and cook. After 15 minutes, add about 2 tablespoons chili powder, 1 bay leaf and garlic powder and pepper to taste. Continue cooking another 45 minutes. Before serving, remove bay leaf and garnish with finely chopped celery, green pepper and/or grated cheddar.

■ Basic hamburgers can be spiced up by serving them with a selection of international condiments: Mexican hot sauce, Chinese soy sauce, Japanese teriyaki sauce, German mustard and of course, American catsup.

KINDEST CUTS OF ALL

Starting at the shoulder of our steer, we come to the prize grilling and broiling candidates:

FIRST CUT CHUCK STEAK (*Blade*). This economical, flavorful cut sits right next to the standing rib roast and contains a large piece of the delicious rib-eye muscle. If you buy a three-inch-thick steak and study it for a moment, you'll spot the round rib eye sitting against the curved rib bone on a corner of the cut. With a small sharp knife, trim out the rib eye, cut it in half horizontally and you have two generous servings of steak (sometimes dubbed Spencer). Buried in the remaining chunk of meat is the wide, flat shoulder blade bone. The long muscle above the bone is fairly tender and excellent thinly sliced for stir-frying. The meat below the bone is tough but tasty and fine for braising.

RIB, RIB EYE (*Delmonico, Spencer, Market, Beauty*). Now we come to the rib area, the tenderest part. Rib steak has the bone in, while rib eye is boneless. You can cut four thick, bone-in steaks from a four-bone standing rib roast. If boneless rib is your passion, buy a rib-eye roast and cut it yourself. You may save up to $1 a pound. If you prefer the flavor of rib eye to that of filet mignon, substitute rib eye in any recipe calling for fillets or tournedos. (Delmonico is a fashionable name given to more than one cut of beef.)

SKIRT (*Butcher Steak*). A long, narrow muscle that lies inside the ribs below the rib roast. It has excellent flavor and lends itself to marinating. To make it tender, you must slice it thin on a slant after cooking. (There is but one per side, and it's often a cut the butcher keeps for himself.)

TOP LOIN (*New York Strip, Kansas City Strip, Shell, Strip, Delmonico, Club*). By any other name, this is one of the greats. Coming from the short loin, this lazy muscle remains tender. Because it has flavor and is just the right size for one portion, top loin is the one most people reach out for. As with the standing rib, you can buy a top loin roast and divide it according to your needs.

T-BONE, PORTERHOUSE. Cut from the short loin, these both consist of a piece of the tenderloin and the top loin divided by a T-shape bone. T-bone has less of the tenderloin than porterhouse. All the pluses of top loin apply here. A T-bone or porterhouse will feed two people.

KINDEST CUTS OF ALL

TENDERLOIN (*Filet Mignon, Tournedos, Chateaubriand, Fillet, Stroganoff Cubes*). We are still looking at the short loin with the large end of the tenderloin joining the sirloin. This tender cut must be purchased well aged for robust flavor. Filet mignon is cut in two-inch-thick pieces from the small end of the tenderloin (closest to the rib); tournedos are cut one and one-quarter inches thick from the center; chateaubriand is a six- to eight-inch piece cut from the center; fillets and stroganoff cubes often come from the large end.

TOP SIRLOIN. This is taken from the sirloin, the next cut back from the short loin, and although not heavily marbled or richly flavored, it is very tender. Cut one and one-quarter inches thick, a top sirloin serves two or three people.

The top sirloin muscle becomes larger as it gets farther away from the short loin. There is a ratio operating here—the larger the muscle, the less tender the meat.

SIRLOIN (*Pin Bone, Flat Bone, Round Bone, Wedge Bone*). Let's take these in the order that they are cut, starting at the end of the short loin and moving back to the tail. Just remember, the farther away the meat gets from the short loin, the less tender. All sirloins will serve three to four people.

Pin bone sirloin looks like a porterhouse steak with an extra bone, shaped like a long thin triangle. Very tender and with good flavor.

Flat bone sirloin is next. It has the T-shape bone removed and a smaller bone that looks like an elongated 8 remaining. Flat bone has fine flavor and is quite tender.

Now we get to round bone sirloin (with its small round bone). This piece is less tender than flat bone but still suitable for grilling.

Last is the wedge bone sirloin (with a small triangular bone). Gristle has entered the picture; although this steak could be broiled, it will be a bit chewy.

KINDEST CUTS OF ALL

BROILABLE BUT...

These members of the steak family can be marinated and broiled, but they are often braised or stewed.

BOTTOM SIRLOIN (*Rump, Sirloin Tip, Essex, Family Steak*). We are now at the inner thigh of the beef and this boneless steak comes from a triangular-shaped cut sometimes called a sirloin tip. The portion right next to the sirloin is tender and flavorful. The cut closer to the round should be braised.

You can buy a rump or sirloin tip roast and cut steaks from the first four inches on the large side, using the remainder for pot roast.

FLANK STEAK. The original London broil. This long, lean, flavorful section lies beneath the short loin and sirloin portion of the steer. It broils beautifully, takes well to marinating and should be sliced thinly on the diagonal across the grain. There's only one flank per side of beef.

TOP ROUND. The largest and tenderest muscle from the round (leg of the steer). Lightly marbled and flavorful (if well aged), the top round is constantly mistreated by meat cutters, who usually slice it quite thin and often mislabel it London broil. If you buy a top round roast and cut it into one and one-quarter-inch-thick steaks, the result will be a very economical feast. Marinate if broiling, or braise.

BOTTOM ROUND. Tougher than top round and excellent for stewing.

EYE OF ROUND. Overpriced and lacks flavor. Fine for stewing, but why use it when chuck or bottom round tastes better and costs less!

Veal

VEAL BREAST STUFFED WITH CORN BREAD AND SAUSAGE

Ask your butcher to make a "pocket" in the veal breast for you.

4 SERVINGS

1 tablespoon olive oil
1 pound sweet Italian sausage, casings removed
1 cup chopped celery
1 cup chopped onion
3 cups 3-day-old corn bread crumbs
½ teaspoon dried red pepper flakes
½ teaspoon salt
½ teaspoon freshly ground pepper
2 eggs, beaten to blend
½ cup pine nuts, toasted (about 2½ ounces)
1 4-pound veal breast, trimmed, with pocket
2 tablespoons dried basil, crumbled
1 teaspoon dried rosemary, crumbled
8 tablespoons white wine vinegar
1¼ cups chicken stock

Heat 1 tablespoon oil in heavy large skillet over medium-high heat. Add sausage, celery and onion and cook until brown, stirring frequently, about 12 minutes. Transfer mixture to large bowl. Add corn bread crumbs, red pepper flakes, salt and pepper. Mix in eggs and pine nuts. Set stuffing aside.

Position rack in center of oven and preheat to 400°F. Arrange veal bone side down to work surface. Fill pocket with stuffing. Close with skewer. Place any remaining stuffing in small baking dish; cover with foil. Place veal in large roasting pan. Rub outside with basil and rosemary. Sprinkle with 3 tablespoons vinegar. Roast veal 30 minutes.

Reduce oven temperature to 350°F. Combine remaining 5 tablespoons vinegar with chicken stock. Continue roasting veal 2 hours, basting every 30 minutes with stock mixture and pan drippings. (Place stuffing in baking dish in oven for last 30 minutes.)

Transfer veal to heated platter. Slice thinly. Serve with any extra stuffing.

OSSO BUCO

2 GENEROUS SERVINGS

3 tablespoons butter

1 finely chopped onion
¼ cup thinly sliced carrots
¼ cup chopped celery
1 minced garlic clove

3 pounds veal shanks
Salt and pepper
Flour
¼ cup olive oil

⅔ cup white wine
½ cup beef stock
¼ teaspoon basil

¼ teaspoon thyme
2 peeled and seeded tomatoes, chopped
1 bay leaf

Cooked noodles (optional)

Melt butter in a small ovenproof casserole. Add onion, carrots, celery and garlic and sauté over moderate heat 10 minutes, stirring frequently. Set aside.

Season veal shanks with salt and pepper and dust them with flour. Heat oil in an 8-inch skillet and brown veal shanks evenly. Add to casserole.

Preheat oven to 350°F. Pour most of the oil from the skillet; add wine and bring to boil, stirring to loosen bits of meat left in the pan. Boil until wine is reduced by half. Stir in the stock, basil, thyme, tomatoes and bay leaf. Bring to a boil and pour over meat and vegetables. Place casserole over direct heat and bring to boil. Cover and bake in oven 1¼ hours or until meat is fork-tender, basting occasionally. Discard bay leaf

and serve the Osso Buco alone or on flat Italian noodles.

VEAL WITH LEEKS AND CREAM

2 SERVINGS

2 tablespoons (¼ stick) butter
2 large leeks (white and pale green parts only), chopped
1 teaspoon chopped fresh thyme or ¼ teaspoon dried, crumbled
6 veal scallops
Salt and pepper
½ cup whipping cream
Sliced green onions (garnish)

Melt 1 tablespoon butter in heavy large skillet over medium heat. Add leeks and thyme and sauté until leeks are tender and just beginning to brown, about 8 minutes. Transfer to small bowl. Increase heat to high. Melt remaining 1 tablespoon butter in same skillet. Season veal with salt and pepper. Add to skillet and cook until

brown and tender, about 2 minutes per side. Transfer veal to platter; cover with foil and keep warm. Add cream and leeks to skillet and boil until reduced to sauce consistency, scraping up any browned bits, about 2 minutes. Season sauce to taste with salt and pepper. Pour sauce over veal. Garnish with green onion slices and serve.

Lamb

BARBECUED SADDLE OF LAMB

This recipe can be adapted for a smaller leg of lamb (bone in). Adjust the ingredient amounts accordingly, and cook as described, or in a 450°F oven. Roast 15 minutes, then reduce oven temperature to 350°F and continue roasting 10 minutes per pound for medium rare.

24 SERVINGS

1 22-pound saddle of lamb
10 large garlic cloves, slivered
½ cup olive oil (preferably Greek), or more
½ cup fresh lemon juice, or more
¼ cup minced fresh oregano, or more
Salt and freshly ground pepper

Prepare barbecue grill with rotisserie attachment. Secure lamb on rotisserie skewer. Insert garlic slivers in meaty part of lamb and under skin; *do not pierce skin.* Gradually whisk olive oil into lemon juice. Brush meat generously with some of mixture. Combine oregano and salt and pepper. Rub mixture into meat. Sprinkle with additional oregano if desired. Roast lamb until meat thermometer inserted in thickest portion of meat registers desired degree of doneness, about 130°F for medium rare (about 3 hours), basting with remaining oil and juice every 20 minutes. Add more olive oil and lemon juice if necessary. Let lamb stand 15 minutes before carving.

MINTY LAMB CHOPS

4 SERVINGS

⅓ cup chopped fresh mint
1 garlic clove, minced
Juice of 1 lemon
½ cup olive oil
Salt and pepper

8 loin lamb chops
Herb Butter*

Combine first 5 ingredients in food processor or blender. Pour over lamb chops. Marinate overnight at room temperature, turning once.

When ready to broil, remove chops from marinade. Blot on paper towels and broil until desired doneness is reached. Serve each chop with Herb Butter.

*HERB BUTTER

½ cup (1 stick) butter, room temperature
2 tablespoons minced fresh mint
1 tablespoon minced parsley
2 garlic cloves, minced

Blend all ingredients. Chill.

YORKSHIRE DEVILED SHOULDER OF LAMB

Accompany each serving with a bit of the savory deviled crust and some sausage stuffing. Offer a tart plum, quince or red currant jam alongside.

6 TO 8 SERVINGS

SAUSAGE STUFFING

1 pound bulk sausage
2 tablespoons (¼ stick) butter
½ cup minced onion
⅓ cup chopped mixed fresh herbs
    (such as parsley, thyme and
    mint)
1 teaspoon dried sage
1 cup fresh breadcrumbs
⅓ cup dry sherry
1 egg, lightly beaten
    Grated peel of 1 lemon
    Salt and freshly ground pepper

1 4- to 5-pound lamb shoulder,
    boned,* room temperature
½ lemon

2 tablespoons seasoning flour,**
    or more

DEVILED CRUST

½ cup fresh breadcrumbs
3 tablespoons English *or* Dijon
    mustard
1 tablespoon vegetable oil
1 teaspoon paprika
½ teaspoon mace
½ teaspoon freshly grated nutmeg
½ teaspoon salt
¼ teaspoon ground red pepper
1 garlic clove, pressed
    Juice and grated peel of
    1 medium lemon

    Fresh watercress sprigs (garnish)
    Additional dry sherry (optional)
    Lamb *or* beef stock (optional)

FOR SAUSAGE STUFFING: Cook sausage in nonstick large skillet over medium heat until fat is rendered, 5 to 6 minutes. Discard fat. Transfer sausage to large bowl. Melt butter in same skillet over low heat. Stir in onion, cover and cook until translucent, about 10 minutes. Remove from heat. Add fresh herbs and sage to onion and toss gently to blend. Add breadcrumbs, sherry, egg, lemon peel, salt and pepper and onion mixture to sausage and blend well; mixture should hold together. Let cool.

Preheat oven to 350°F. Spread stuffing evenly over boned lamb. Roll into log shape, fat side out, and tie with string at 2-inch intervals. Rub entire surface with cut side of lemon. Sprinkle evenly with seasoning flour, using enough to cover entire surface. Transfer lamb to parchment-paper-lined roasting pan. Roast uncovered 1 hour.

FOR DEVILED CRUST: Mix all ingredients in small bowl and set aside.

Remove lamb from oven and coat entire surface with crust mixture. Return to oven and continue roasting until crust is golden and lamb is tender, pink and juicy, about 1 hour. Transfer to heated platter. Let stand 10 to 15 minutes before cutting into thick slices. Garnish each serving with watercress sprigs. Deglaze pan juices with additional sherry and stock. Reduce juices to saucelike consistency and serve.

*Lamb shoulder with bone in can be substituted. Make long slashes across surface of meat, spacing cuts about 1 inch apart. Rub with lemon, then sprinkle with seasoning flour. Cut pocket large enough to contain stuffing under fatty surface. Continue as described in recipe instructions.

**For seasoning flour, combine 2 tablespoons all purpose flour, 1 teaspoon salt and ½ teaspoon freshly ground pepper in small cup. Makes about 2½ tablespoons.

PARISIAN LAMB STEW WITH WHITE BEANS

If you prefer a thicker stew, purée some of the beans and reblend into stew.

6 TO 8 SERVINGS

3 cups dried white pea (navy) beans

4 pounds boneless lamb stew meat, patted dry
Salt and freshly ground pepper
¼ cup olive oil
2 onions, chopped
4 garlic cloves, minced
2 tablespoons all purpose flour
4 cups chicken or beef stock
1 bouquet garni (bay leaf, parsley, celery leaves, ½ teaspoon dried thyme and 1 strip lemon peel, tied together in a cheesecloth bag)
2 tomatoes, peeled, seeded and chopped
1 tablespoon soy sauce
Juice of 1 lemon
1 teaspoon dried rosemary or thyme
2 parsley sprigs
¼ cup minced fresh parsley

Place beans in large pot and cover with salted water. Bring to boil over high heat. Cook 2 minutes. Remove from heat, cover and let stand 1 hour. Drain well. Cover beans with fresh water. Cover and simmer until tender, at least 1 hour. Drain beans thoroughly.

Season lamb with salt and pepper. Heat oil in large Dutch oven or heavy large saucepan over medium-high heat. Add lamb in batches and brown on all sides. Remove lamb from saucepan using slotted spoon. Reduce heat to low, add onions and garlic to same saucepan and cook 2 minutes. Add flour and cook until well browned, stirring constantly. Blend in stock, bouquet garni, tomatoes, soy sauce, lemon juice, rosemary and parsley sprigs. Return lamb to saucepan. Add beans and bring to boil. Reduce heat, cover and simmer until meat is tender, about 1½ to 2 hours. Skim fat from sauce. Discard bouquet garni. Season to taste with salt and pepper. Sprinkle with minced fresh parsley and serve.

Pork

SWEET-AND-SOUR SPARERIBS

3 TO 4 SERVINGS

2½ to 3 pounds meaty pork spareribs
Salt and pepper

SAUCE

¼ cup firmly packed dark brown
  sugar
3 tablespoons lemon juice
1 small jar strained apricots,
  apricots-and-applesauce or pears
1½ teaspoons molasses
1½ teaspoons dark corn syrup
½ teaspoon ground ginger
  Dash of hot pepper sauce
¼ cup chili sauce
1 small garlic clove, pressed
1 tablespoon soy sauce
½ teaspoon dry mustard

Sprinkle ribs with salt and pepper. Broil
3 to 5 minutes per side. Place in 9x13-inch
baking dish.

FOR SAUCE: Mix all ingredients in
1-quart pan. Heat briefly on medium-low,
stirring until combined. Reduce oven
to 350°F. Pour half the sauce over ribs
and bake uncovered 30 minutes. Pour
remaining sauce over spareribs and
continue baking for another 30 minutes.

STUFFED PORK CHOPS

4 SERVINGS

1 cup mixed dried fruit, cut up
¼ cup raisins
1 cup white wine
2 cups herb stuffing mix
¼ cup diced celery
2 tablespoons diced onion
¼ cup (½ stick) butter, melted
  Water
  Salt and freshly ground pepper
4 rib pork chops, 1½ inches thick
  (slit pocket in each)

Preheat oven to 350°F. Plump mixed fruit
and raisins in wine; drain, reserving wine.
Combine fruit, stuffing mix, celery and
onion. Pour melted butter over and stir.
Add water to moisten as desired and
blend well. Taste and add salt and pepper
as needed. Stuff each chop; lightly pack
remaining stuffing in small casserole.
Place meat in baking dish, add reserved
wine, cover with foil and bake 30 minutes. Remove foil and continue baking
30 minutes with remaining dressing.

BUTCHER'S ONE-POT WITH SAUERKRAUT (SCHLÄCHTTOPF MIT SAUERKRAUT)

5 SERVINGS

3 thick slices bacon (preferably
  country cured), cut in half
½ pound small country sausages
1 large onion, chopped

1 medium carrot, finely diced
1 tablespoon minced fresh parsley
2 pounds canned sauerkraut,
   rinsed and drained
10 juniper berries, crushed
⅔ cup water
½ cup dry German white wine
1 large bay leaf, bruised
¾ teaspoon caraway seeds
¼ teaspoon freshly ground pepper
4 medium potatoes, peeled and cut
   into ¼-inch slices
   Salt and freshly ground pepper

1 pound assorted German sausages
   (blockwurst, wienerwurst,
   blutwurst and knockwurst)
1 tablespoon snipped fresh chives

Cook bacon in large Dutch oven or flameproof casserole over medium-high heat until crisp. Remove with slotted spoon and drain on paper towels. Add country sausages to same pan and brown thoroughly on all sides. Remove with slotted spoon and drain.

Combine onion, carrot and parsley in same pan and cook over medium heat 4 to 5 minutes. Add sauerkraut, juniper berries, water, wine, bay leaf, caraway seeds and ¼ teaspoon pepper and mix well. Reduce heat to low. Arrange potatoes over sauerkraut and season lightly with salt and pepper. Top potatoes with bacon slices and country sausages. Cover and cook gently over low heat about 20 minutes, watching carefully to prevent sticking.

Just before serving, arrange assorted sausages over top of casserole. Cover and cook until sausages are lightly steamed (*do not allow to split*), about 10 minutes. Transfer to soup tureen or serve from Dutch oven. Sprinkle with chives and serve immediately.

GOULASH WITH WINE-BRAISED SAUERKRAUT

This Hungarian stew can be prepared ahead and reheated before serving. It goes well with boiled potatoes dusted with fresh dill, a salad of romaine with thin slices of sweet red onion and a loaf of warm black bread.

8 SERVINGS

2 pounds sauerkraut (fresh, canned
   or packaged)

2 tablespoons vegetable oil
2 onions, chopped
3 to 4 tablespoons Hungarian sweet
   paprika
2 garlic cloves, minced
1 cup dry white wine
3½ pounds boneless pork stew meat,
   cut into 1-inch cubes
1½ teaspoons caraway seeds
¼ cup tomato purée
2 cups chicken broth

½ cup whipping cream
½ cup sour cream

2 tablespoons all purpose flour
Salt and freshly ground pepper
Minced fresh parsley (optional
garnish)

Thoroughly rinse sauerkraut under cold running water and drain well. Transfer to large bowl. Cover with cold water and let stand 20 minutes, changing water once. Squeeze sauerkraut to remove as much water as possible and set aside.

Heat oil in Dutch oven or large flameproof casserole over medium heat. Add onions and paprika and cook, stirring occasionally, until onions are limp and pale gold, about 10 minutes. Add garlic and cook 1 to 2 more minutes. Stir in ½ cup wine and bring mixture to boil. Add pork. Place sauerkraut over pork. Sprinkle caraway seeds over top. Combine tomato purée and remaining wine in small bowl and whisk well. Stir tomato mixture and broth into pot. Bring mixture to boil. Reduce heat, cover and simmer, stirring occasionally and adding more liquid if necessary, 1 to 1½ hours.

Remove pork and sauerkraut from pot and keep warm. Combine cream, sour cream and flour in small bowl, blending well. Whisk cream mixture into sauce and cook over low heat, stirring constantly, 10 minutes. Return pork and sauerkraut to pot, blending well. Season with salt and pepper to taste. Ladle goulash into shallow bowls or rimmed plates. Sprinkle with parsley if desired and serve.

Poultry

TURKEY CUTLETS WITH PAPRIKA CREAM SAUCE
Offer purchased pound cake for dessert.

2 SERVINGS;
CAN BE DOUBLED OR TRIPLED

2 tablespoons (¼ stick) butter
½ onion, chopped
1 teaspoon paprika
½ cup whipping cream
1 teaspoon Dijon mustard
2 teaspoons minced fresh dill
Salt and pepper

¾ pound turkey breast cutlets
All purpose flour

Melt 1 tablespoon butter in heavy medium skillet over medium heat. Add onion and sauté until tender, about 8 minutes. Add paprika and stir 1 minute. Add cream. Simmer until slightly thickened, about 1 minute. Mix in mustard and dill. Season sauce with salt and pepper. Cover and set aside.

Season turkey with salt and pepper. Dredge in flour. Melt remaining 1 tablespoon butter in heavy large skillet over medium-high heat. Add turkey and sauté until just cooked through, about 1 minute per side. Transfer to plates. Spoon sauce over and serve.

ROAST CHICKEN WITH ROSEMARY BUTTER

A vertical roaster cuts cooking time by at least 25 percent and requires little attention.

2 SERVINGS (PLUS ENCORE)

1 small garlic clove, minced
3 tablespoons (⅜ stick) unsalted butter, room temperature
Juice of 1 lemon
2 tablespoons fresh rosemary or 2 teaspoons dried leaves, crumbled
¼ teaspoon salt
⅛ teaspoon freshly ground pepper
1 2½- to 3-pound frying chicken, rinsed and patted dry
½ lemon
Paprika (Hungarian preferred)
½ cup water

If using vertical roaster, place rack in lowest portion and preheat oven to 450°F. Combine garlic, butter, lemon juice, rosemary, salt and pepper in processor or blender and mix well (lemon may not blend in completely). Stuff mixture under skin of chicken in breast and thigh areas. Rub skin with cut lemon and sprinkle with paprika.

Set on vertical roaster (or on rack) in shallow roasting pan. Add water to pan and roast chicken 15 minutes. Reduce oven to 375°F and continue roasting until chicken is done (allow about 15 minutes to the pound if using vertical roaster, or about 20 minutes to the pound if using regular rack). To serve, cut into quarters.

MAHOGANY CHICKEN WINGS

20 SERVINGS

1½ cups soy sauce
¾ cup dry sherry
1⅛ cups hoisin sauce*
¾ cup Chinese plum sauce*
18 green onions, minced
6 large garlic cloves, minced
¾ cup cider vinegar
½ cup honey

6 to 7 pounds chicken wings

In 3-quart saucepan, combine all ingredients except wings. Bring to a boil and simmer 5 minutes. Cool.

While sauce is cooling, cut off wing tips and set aside for stockpot. Disjoint wings and place in large storage container. Pour cooled sauce over, cover and refrigerate overnight.

Place oven racks in upper and lower thirds of oven and preheat to 375°F. Oil 2 large shallow roasting pans.

Drain wings. Divide between prepared pans and bake uncovered 1 to 1½ hours, basting about every 20 minutes with remaining sauce and turning to brown evenly. Be sure to switch the pans halfway through cooking.

Remove chicken wings from pans and let cool on large sheets of foil. When cool, wrap and store for up to 3 days. Serve at room temperature.

Both of these products are available in Oriental food stores or gourmet shops.

CHICKEN PICCATA

This dish goes well with fettuccini, and cooked chilled broccoli dressed with olive oil and lemon juice and a sprinkling of pine nuts. A chilled Soave or Gewürztraminer is a good wine choice.

4 TO 8 SERVINGS

- 4 whole chicken breasts, skinned, boned and halved
- ½ cup flour
- 1½ teaspoons salt
- ¼ teaspoon freshly ground pepper
  Paprika to taste
- ¼ cup clarified butter
- 1 tablespoon olive oil
- 2 to 4 tablespoons dry Madeira or water
- 3 tablespoons fresh lemon juice
  Lemon slices
- 3 to 4 tablespoons capers (optional)
- ¼ cup minced fresh parsley (optional garnish)

Place chicken breasts between 2 sheets of waxed paper and pound them until thin (about ¼ inch). Combine flour, salt, pepper and paprika in bag. Add breasts and coat well; shake off excess.

Heat butter and olive oil in large skillet until bubbling. Sauté chicken breasts, a few at a time, 2 to 3 minutes on each side. *Do not overcook.* Drain on paper towels and keep warm.

Drain off all but 2 tablespoons of butter and oil. Stir Madeira or water into drippings, scraping bottom of skillet to loosen any browned bits. Add lemon juice and heat briefly. Return chicken to skillet, interspersing with lemon slices, and heat until sauce thickens. Add capers; sprinkle with minced parsley.

BAKED CHICKEN WITH MUSHROOM AND ARTICHOKES

4 SERVINGS

- 4 chicken breast halves
  Salt and pepper
- 1 6-ounce jar marinated artichoke hearts
- 8 ounces mushrooms, sliced
- 5 green onions, chopped
- 1 cup dry white wine

Preheat oven to 350°F. Season chicken breast halves with salt and pepper. Place skin side up in 9x13-inch baking dish. Drain artichokes, reserving marinade. Cut artichokes in half. Top chicken breasts with artichokes, mushrooms and green onions. Pour reserved marinade and white wine over. Bake until chicken is cooked through, about 45 minutes.

GINGER-CASHEW CHICKEN

6 SERVINGS

2 tablespoons plus 1 teaspoon olive oil
4 small onions, sliced
6 garlic cloves, chopped
2 teaspoons minced fresh ginger
2 pounds boneless skinless chicken breasts, cut into ½-inch-thick strips
4 celery stalks, sliced

1 tablespoon all purpose flour
1 cup canned chicken broth
¼ cup dry sherry
3 tablespoons soy sauce
1 teaspoon dry mustard
1 cup salted roasted cashews
3 green onions, sliced (garnish)
    Steamed rice

Heat 2 tablespoons oil in wok or heavy large skillet over high heat. Add onions and cook until tender, stirring frequently, about 10 minutes. Add garlic and ginger and continue cooking until onions are golden brown, about 5 minutes. Add chicken and celery and cook until chicken is cooked through, stirring occasionally, about 7 minutes. Transfer mixture to platter. Set aside.

Add remaining teaspoon oil to wok. Add flour and stir over medium-high heat until just beginning to color, about 1 minute. Mix in broth, sherry, soy sauce and mustard. Boil until slightly thickened, stirring frequently, about 5 minutes. Return chicken mixture to wok. Mix in cashews. Cook until chicken is heated through, about 3 minutes. Transfer to platter. Garnish with green onions and serve with rice.

CHICKEN WITH MUSHROOMS AND CREAM

An easy entrée for weekend entertaining or an elegant midweek dinner.

4 SERVINGS

3 tablespoons butter
1 chicken (about 3½ pounds), cut into 8 pieces
    Salt and pepper
¾ pound mushrooms, sliced
½ cup chopped onion
2 tablespoons all purpose flour
2 14½-ounce cans low-salt chicken broth
1 cup whipping cream
½ teaspoon dried rosemary, crumbled

Melt butter in Dutch oven or casserole over medium-high heat. Season chicken generously with salt and pepper. Add to Dutch oven and cook until golden brown, turning occasionally, about 8 minutes. Remove chicken. Add mushrooms and onion to Dutch oven and sauté until mushrooms are golden brown, about 6 minutes. Sprinkle mushrooms and onion with flour and stir over medium heat 2 minutes. Mix in chicken broth, cream and rosemary. Boil until liquid thickens slightly, about 10 minutes. Return chicken to Dutch oven. Cook until chicken is tender, about 25 minutes. Transfer chicken to platter. Boil liquid until reduced to sauce, about 10 minutes. Spoon sauce over chicken and serve.

Fish

JAMBALAYA

20 SERVINGS

¼ cup oil
¼ cup (½ stick) butter
6 cups chopped green onions (about 6 bunches)
5 cups chopped onions (about 2¼ pounds)
1½ cups chopped celery including leaves (about 3½ stalks)
1½ cups chopped green pepper (about 1½ peppers)
1 pound raw shrimp, shelled, deveined and minced
¾ pound ham, minced
⅓ cup minced garlic
2 quarts (8 cups) canned tomatoes, thoroughly drained, coarsely chopped
½ cup tomato paste
2 tablespoons basil

2 tablespoons marjoram
1½ tablespoons thyme
1½ teaspoons oregano
¾ to 1 teaspoon cayenne
¾ teaspoon cloves
2 bay leaves

8 cups chicken stock or broth
4 cups long-grain converted rice
2¼ pounds ham, cut into ¾-inch chunks
Salt and freshly ground pepper
6 pounds raw medium shrimp, shelled and deveined*

Heat oil and butter in 8-quart pot. Add all onions, celery, green pepper, minced shrimp and ham; sauté over medium-high heat until soft, about 5 minutes. Add garlic and cook 1 more minute.

Stir in tomatoes, tomato paste, herbs and spices. Reduce heat to medium and continue cooking 10 minutes.

Add stock and bring to boil. Stir in rice, cover and cook over low heat 25 to 30 minutes, until rice is tender and most of liquid is absorbed. Stir in ham chunks and season to taste with salt and pepper. (A bit more cayenne and basil or thyme may also be needed.) *Jambalaya may be refrigerated up to 3 days at this point.*

Preheat oven to 350°F. Transfer jambalaya to 8- to 10-quart casserole or two 4- or 5-quart casseroles. Cover and bake 40 to 50 minutes for large casserole or 30 to 35 for small, or until rice is hot. Stir in shrimp, cover and bake until shrimp are firm, about 10 minutes. Serve hot, directly from casserole.

*If preparing jambalaya ahead, purchase 6 pounds of raw shrimp the day recipe is to be completed and served.

GRILLED SALMON STEAKS WITH LIME BUTTER

4 SERVINGS

½ cup (1 stick) butter, melted
¼ cup lime juice
1 tablespoon pepper
4 9-ounce salmon steaks
Lime wedges

Combine first 3 ingredients. Place salmon in glass baking dish. Pour lime butter over. Let salmon marinate while preparing barbecue or preheating broiler.

Prepare barbecue (medium-high heat) or preheat broiler. Cook salmon until just opaque, brushing with lime butter marinade occasionally, about 4 minutes per side. Transfer to plates. Brush with any remaining lime butter. Serve immediately with lime wedges.

SWORDFISH KEBABS

4 SERVINGS

1½ pounds swordfish, cut into ¾-inch cubes
1 14-ounce can hearts of palm, drained, cut into ½-inch-thick slices
1 zucchini, cut into ½-inch-thick slices
1 red bell pepper, cut into ¾-inch pieces
½ cup ranch-style salad dressing
Salt and pepper

Prepare barbecue (medium-high heat) or preheat broiler. Alternate swordfish with hearts of palm, zucchini and bell pepper on metal skewers. Brush with dressing. Season with salt and pepper. Grill until cooked through, about 10 minutes.

BAKED SALMON WITH CHAMPAGNE AND DILL MAYONNAISE

If you're running short on time, purchased mayonnaise can be substituted for the homemade. Just mix two cups mayonnaise with a little lemon juice and some minced fresh dill. Offer the choice of a Napa Valley Chardonnay or Syrah.

10 SERVINGS

MAYONNAISE

4 egg yolks
2 tablespoons fresh lemon juice
4 teaspoons Dijon mustard

1½ cups vegetable oil
Salt and freshly ground pepper
10 tablespoons chopped fresh dill

SALMON

Olive oil
1 6-pound whole salmon, scaled
   and cleaned, head and tail intact
Freshly ground pepper
1 small bunch fresh dill, large
   stems trimmed
¼ cup (½ stick) butter, cut into
   pieces

½ cup Champagne or other
   sparkling wine

FOR MAYONNAISE: Blend yolks, lemon juice and mustard in processor. Gradually add oil in slow steady stream, blending until thick. Season with salt and pepper. Add dill and blend until just combined. Transfer to bowl. (*Can be prepared 2 days ahead. Cover and refrigerate. Let stand 30 minutes at room temperature before using.*)

FOR SALMON: Preheat oven to 400°F.

Grease large rimmed cookie sheet with olive oil. Brush salmon inside and out with oil. Season inside and out with pepper. Arrange dill in cavity. Top dill with butter pieces. Bake until salmon near backbone is no longer translucent (make small cut along backbone to check), about 30 minutes.

Increase oven temperature to 500°F. Pour Champagne over fish. Bake 5 minutes more. Remove from oven. Tent salmon with foil and let stand 15 minutes. Slide fish off cookie sheet and onto platter using metal spatula as aid. Peel skin off. Serve, passing mayonnaise separately.

BAKED RED SNAPPER WITH DILL SAUCE

2 SERVINGS

⅓ cup mayonnaise
1 garlic clove, minced
½ teaspoon fresh lemon juice
½ teaspoon minced green onion

½ teaspoon minced fresh dill or
   pinch of dried dill weed
Pinch of ground pepper

1 lemon, sliced
2 green onions, sliced
2 fresh dill sprigs or 1 teaspoon
   dried dill weed
1 12-ounce red snapper fillet
Salt and pepper
Additional fresh dill sprigs
   (optional garnish)

Combine mayonnaise, garlic, lemon juice, green onion, dill and ground pepper in small bowl. Set sauce aside.

Preheat oven to 400°F. Place lemon slices in center of large sheet of foil. Top with sliced green onions and dill sprigs. Place fish atop onions and dill. Season with salt and pepper. Fold foil tightly to make packet. Place on baking sheet and cook until fish is opaque, about 20 minutes. Remove fish from packet. Garnish snapper with dill if desired. Pass sauce separately.

Pastas, Pizzas & Sandwiches

Toothsome pastas dripping with sauces or stuffed with fillings of tomato, cream, or cheese. Crisp pizzas generously topped with pepperoni and mozzarella or fresh garden vegetables. Sandwiches of crusty bread piled high with succulent chicken and sausage or delicate crabmeat salad. The following time-honored recipes for an array of universal favorites prove that fun food can be food that is good for you, too.

Pasta

LINGUINE WITH TOMATO-BASIL SAUCE

This is a robust sauce that tastes of summer. If in season, use fresh tomatoes and basil. The sauce will keep in the refrigerator 4 to 5 days, or may be frozen up to 4 months. Make it in quanity as it lends itself to delicious variations.

4 TO 6 MAIN-COURSE SERVINGS
OR 6 TO 8 FIRST-COURSE SERVINGS

¼ cup full-bodied olive oil
2 medium onions, chopped
1 large garlic clove, minced
1 28-ounce can tomatoes, undrained, seeded and chopped, or 2 pounds fresh tomatoes, peeled, seeded and chopped
1½ to 2 tablespoons dried basil or ¼ cup fresh
½ teaspoon dried oregano or 1½ teaspoons fresh
1 to 1½ teaspoons sugar
Salt and freshly ground pepper
1 pound linguine, cooked al dente
Freshly grated imported Parmesan cheese

Heat oil in large heavy skillet over medium-low heat. Add onion and cook until soft and transparent, about 10 minutes. Add garlic and cook an additional 2 minutes. Blend in tomatoes and herbs. Increase heat to high, bring to boil and cook until some of liquid has evaporated, about 5 minutes. Add sugar, salt and pepper to taste. Add pasta and toss until blended. Serve immediately with Parmesan cheese.

FETTUCCINE WITH PEAS AND HAM

6 TO 8 SERVINGS

5 tablespoons (⅝ stick) unsalted butter
6 shallots, minced
½ pound mushrooms, sliced
1¼ cups whipping cream
1 10-ounce package frozen tiny peas, thawed
4 ounces boiled ham, chopped
1 cup freshly grated imported Parmesan cheese
1 pound fettuccine, cooked al dente and drained
Salt and freshly ground pepper

Additional freshly grated Parmesan (optional)

Heat butter in heavy large nonaluminum skillet. Add shallots and sauté until soft. Add mushrooms, increase heat to high and cook until mushrooms are very lightly browned. Add cream and let boil 2 minutes. Stir in peas and cook about 30 seconds. Reduce heat to low; blend in ham, cheese and fettuccine and toss until heated, well combined and sauce clings to pasta. Season to taste with salt and generous amount of pepper. Turn into heated platter and serve. Pass additional cheese, if desired.

Sauce can be prepared an hour or so ahead to point of adding peas.

SPINACH- AND CHEESE-STUFFED PASTA SHELLS

Fennel seeds add a flavorful new twist to this vegetarian main course.

6 SERVINGS

2 10-ounce packages frozen chopped spinach, thawed
15 ounces ricotta cheese
1 cup (about 4 ounces) grated Parmesan
2 tablespoons fennel seeds
2 tablespoons chopped fresh basil or 2 teaspoons dried, crumbled
3 garlic cloves, minced
Salt and pepper
3½ cups purchased marinara or spaghetti sauce
32 jumbo pasta shells, freshly cooked

Additional grated Parmesan

Squeeze spinach dry. Transfer spinach to large bowl. Add ricotta, ½ cup Parmesan, fennel, basil and garlic to bowl. Season mixture with salt and pepper; blend.

Preheat oven to 350°F. Spoon ½ cup marinara sauce evenly over bottom of 9x13x2-inch baking dish. Fill each pasta shell with spinach mixture. Place shells, filling side up, in dish. Spoon remaining sauce over shells. Sprinkle with remaining ½ cup Parmesan. Cover loosely with foil and bake until heated through, about 30 minutes. Serve, passing additional Parmesan separately.

SPAGHETTI WITH ONION AND GARLIC

4 TO 6 SERVINGS

½ cup olive oil
1 medium onion, chopped
2 garlic cloves, minced
¼ cup water
Salt and pepper
1 pound spaghetti, freshly cooked
Grated Parmesan

Heat oil in heavy large skillet over medium heat. Add onion and garlic and sauté until light brown, 6 minutes. Let cool slightly.

Add ¼ cup water to skillet and mix well. Season with salt and pepper. Return spaghetti to pot in which it was cooked; pour sauce over. Place over low heat and toss until heated through. Sprinkle with Parmesan. Serve immediately.

THREE-PEPPER LINGUINE

4 SERVINGS

2 tablespoons olive oil
1 large green bell pepper, coarsely chopped
1 large red bell pepper, coarsely chopped
1 large yellow bell pepper, coarsely chopped

½ onion, chopped
2 garlic cloves, minced
1 cup canned Italian-style plum
   tomatoes, drained and chopped

9 ounces spinach linguine, freshly
   cooked
½ cup prepared pesto
   Grated Parmesan

Heat oil in heavy large skillet over medium heat. Add bell peppers, onion and garlic and sauté until soft, 6 minutes. Stir in tomatoes and simmer 7 minutes.

Toss linguine with pesto. Divide evenly among 4 plates. Spoon bell pepper sauce over. Sprinkle with Parmesan and serve.

OLD FASHIONED SPAGHETTI AND MEATBALLS

2 TO 4 SERVINGS

½ pound ground beef
1 egg

1½ slices white bread, torn into small
   pieces
2 tablespoons grated Parmesan
   Salt and pepper
¼ cup olive oil

1½ cups Marinara Sauce (see recipe)
8 ounces spaghetti, freshly cooked
   Additional grated Parmesan

Combine first 4 ingredients in medium bowl. Season with salt and pepper. Form mixture into 1½-inch-diameter meatballs. Heat oil in heavy large skillet over medium-high heat. Add meatballs in batches (do not crowd) and cook until brown on all sides, about 8 minutes.

Meanwhile, warm Marinara Sauce in heavy small saucepan over low heat. Pour sauce over spaghetti. Top with meatballs. Serve immediately, passing additional Parmesan separately.

MARINARA SAUCE

A simple all-purpose tomato sauce that's perfect over pasta as well as meats and seafood. Prepare a double batch and freeze the extra to have for another time.

MAKES ABOUT 1½ CUPS

3 tablespoons olive oil
2 onions, chopped
1 garlic clove, minced
2½ cups peeled, seeded, diced
   tomatoes
¼ teaspoon dried oregano, crumbled
¼ teaspoon sugar
   Pinch of dried basil, crumbled
   Salt and pepper

Heat oil in heavy medium saucepan over medium heat. Add onions and garlic and sauté until translucent, about 5 minutes. Add tomatoes, oregano, sugar and basil and simmer until thickened, stirring occasionally, about 1 hour. Season with salt and pepper.

PASTA POINTERS

Faced with only a few minutes to whip up a meal, an Italian cook will reach into the refrigerator for a dash of this and a bit of that, all the while thinking—pasta!

What shape pasta to use for which sauce? That's simple. Heavier-textured sauces are generally combined with thicker pastas (fusilli, fettuccine, tagliatelle, linguine, shells, ziti etc.). And light or thin sauces are served with the finer pastas (capelli d'angelo, vermicelli, spaghettini, quadrettini etc.).

When it comes to the all-important cooking of the noodle, remember this rule. For every pound of pasta have six quarts of boiling water (with two tablespoons salt added). If cooking very large or filled pastas (ravioli or lasagne for instance), add three tablespoons vegetable oil to the water. Drop the pasta in and boil rapidly, stirring occasionally to avoid sticking, until the noodles are tender but still al dente, a little firm to the bite. This is the only proper way to serve pasta. If it overcooks, throw it out! Drain immediately in a colander, making sure to shake out all liquid.

Ideally combine the pasta with sauce at this point, but there is a way of holding it for several hours before serving. Rinse with hot water to remove starch and drain again. Now toss the noodles with a generous amount of butter or olive oil (whichever will blend well with your chosen sauce) and set aside. Shortly before serving, either toss with the sauce until heated through or place covered in a 350°F oven for 15 minutes and then blend.

Pizza

FAST DEEP-DISH PIZZA

8 SERVINGS

2 28-ounce cans plum tomatoes, drained

2 large garlic cloves, pressed

2 tablespoons chopped fresh parsley

1½ teaspoons dried oregano, crumbled

1 teaspoon dried basil, crumbled

3 teaspoons olive oil
Cornmeal

1 pound (1 loaf) frozen bread dough, thawed

1 pound shredded mozzarella (about 4 cups)

7 ounces thinly sliced pepperoni

½ cup grated Parmesan

Preheat oven to 425°F. Coarsely chop tomatoes. Place in strainer and drain well.

Combine tomatoes with garlic, parsley, oregano and basil in bowl. Brush 12-inch-diameter deep-dish pizza pan with 1 teaspoon oil. Sprinkle pan with cornmeal. Roll bread dough out to 13-inch round on lightly floured surface. Transfer dough to pan, extending 1 inch up pan sides. Spread dough with 1 cup tomato mixture. Sprinkle half of mozzarella over. Top with half of pepperoni and remaining tomato mixture. Sprinkle with remaining mozzarella. Distribute remaining pepperoni atop mozzarella. Sprinkle with Parmesan. Drizzle with remaining 2 teaspoons olive oil. Bake until cheese bubbles and begins to brown and crust is golden brown, about 40 minutes.

VEGETARIAN PIZZA

6 SERVINGS

SAUCE

2 tablespoon olive oil

1 large onion, chopped

1 large tomato, peeled, seeded, chopped

3 large garlic cloves, minced

¼ cup chopped fresh basil
Salt and pepper

PIZZA

Cornmeal

1 1-pound loaf purchased frozen bread dough, thawed

1¾ cups grated provolone cheese (about 7 ounces)

¾ cup freshly grated Parmesan cheese (about 3 ounces)

¼ cup chopped fresh basil

FOR SAUCE: Heat oil in heavy small skillet over medium heat. Add onion and sauté until translucent, about 6 minutes. Add tomato and garlic and cook until liquid evaporates, stirring occasionally, about 10 minutes. Mix in basil. Season to taste with salt and pepper. (*Can be prepared 1 day ahead. Refrigerate.*)

FOR PIZZA: Prepare barbecue (medium-high heat). Place pizza stone on grill and heat 5 minutes. Sprinkle rimless cookie sheet with cornmeal. Roll dough out on floured surface to 11-inch round. Transfer to prepared cookie sheet. Spread sauce over, leaving ½-inch border. Top with cheeses. Slide pizza onto stone on grill. Cover barbecue. Cook pizza until crust is crisp and cheeses melt, about 10 minutes. Sprinkle with basil and serve.

Sandwiches

HOT OPEN-FACE VEGETABLE AND CHEESE SANDWICHES

2 SERVINGS

2 large slices rye sandwich bread
1 avocado, thinly sliced
1 small tomato, thinly sliced
¼ cup plain yogurt
¼ cup drained sliced black olives
3 tablespoons coarsely chopped roasted salted cashews
2 tablespoons minced onion
¼ cup shredded sharp cheddar
¼ cup shredded Monterey Jack cheese
4 ounces mozzarella, cut into 6 slices
Salt and pepper

Preheat broiler. Place bread slices on cookie sheet. Arrange avocado slices on bread. Arrange sliced tomato atop avocado. Spoon 2 tablespoons yogurt onto each sandwich, spreading evenly. Sprinkle with olives, cashews and onion. Top with cheeses. Season with salt and pepper. Broil sandwiches 6 inches from heat source until cheese melts, about 3 minutes. Serve hot.

ROASTED CHICKEN AND SAUSAGE SANDWICHES

Sausage is tucked under the chicken skin to keep the chicken moist during baking. For those who like them, the cooked livers are good added to the sandwiches.

MAKES ABOUT 16

2 3½-pound chickens, livers reserved
Salt and pepper
2 onions, halved
1 bunch fresh basil
1 bunch fresh rosemary
1 pound smoked kielbasa sausage, cut into 4-inch-long pieces, then halved lengthwise
6 tablespoons olive oil

3 French bread baguettes, cut on diagonal into 3-inch-long pieces, halved horizontally

1 cup mayonnaise
4 teaspoons ground cumin

Preheat oven to 375°F. Generously season chicken cavities with salt and pepper. Loosely pack half of onions and half of basil and rosemary into cavity of each. Slide fingers between breast skin and meat to loosen. Place sausage under loosened skin. Halve livers and tuck under skin at joint between thigh and body. Rub oil over chickens. Arrange chickens breast side up on racks in roasting pans.

Roast chickens 30 minutes. Turn breast side down and continue roasting until juices run clear when thighs are pierced with knife, about 30 more minutes. Cool chickens slightly.

Preheat broiler. Arrange bread cut side up on cookie sheet and broil until golden brown. Mix mayonnaise and cumin. Spread mayonnaise mixture over bread. Thinly slice chicken, sausage and livers (if desired). Arrange chicken, sausage and livers atop bottom bread slices. Season with salt and pepper. Cover with top bread slices. Serve warm or at room temperature.

FAST-FOOD DIRECTIONS

JUST ABOUT EVERYONE ON THE GO eats a fast-food meal once in a while. But before you head for the drive-through, take a look at the "Fast Food Eating Guide." This information-packed chart compares the calorie, fat, sodium and sugar content of over 250 popular foods and meals. The poster-size chart folds up easily (great for stowing in the glove compartment) and is available for $4.95 from The Center for Science in the Public Interest, 1875 Connecticut Avenue, NW, no. 300, Washington, DC 20009.

CRAB SALAD PITA

2 SERVINGS

3 tablespoons light mayonnaise
3 tablespoons tarragon vinegar or white wine vinegar
1 teaspoon dried tarragon, crumbled
½ pound lump crabmeat
2 thin slices Canadian bacon or ham, chopped
2 whole wheat pita breads, halved
  Shredded lettuce
  Thinly sliced tomatoes
  Alfalfa sprouts
  Avocado slices

Mix mayonnaise, vinegar and tarragon in medium bowl. Add crabmeat and bacon and stir to combine. Open bread halves, forming pockets. Line each with lettuce. Divide crab salad among pita halves. Top with tomatoes, alfalfa sprouts and avocado.

FILLING PITA POCKETS

When it comes to filling the pita bread, almost anything goes. Arrange the wherewithal on the buffet table. Let your guests make their own combinations. Here are a few suggestions:

- Thinly sliced turkey, chunks of red or green pepper, sour cream and chutney

- Slivers of rare roast beef, sliced cherry tomatoes, chopped green onions, cubes of cream cheese and alfalfa sprouts

- Chopped ham, raw mushroom slices, mustard-flavored mayonnaise and chopped walnuts

- Crisp crumbled bacon, diced avocado tossed with fresh lemon juice, shredded lettuce and sour cream

- Chopped hard-cooked eggs mixed with mayonnaise, minced onion and a little crumbled blue cheese

- Tiny cooked shrimp, asparagus tips and mayonnaise flavored with a bit of tarragon

- Shredded lettuce, chopped red onion, ripe olives, sliced cucumbers, artichoke hearts and tuna lightly coated in a vinaigrette dressing

Eggs & Cheese

Dishes featuring eggs and cheese seem to capture the very essence of old-fashioned, farmhouse goodness. Intended to be served at times of day other than just breakfast or brunch alone, these classic dairy recipes—from Quick Egg-Cheese Soufflé to Mozzarella and Tomato Sauce Omelets, Creamy Zucchini Quiche to Blueberry Blintzes—offer wholesome, satisfying eating at its best.

Frittata di Zucchine (Italian Egg Pancake with Zucchini)

A frittata, unlike a French omelet, must cook slowly over low heat until well done, but should be neither tough nor dry.

6 SERVINGS

2 tablespoons imported olive oil
1 large garlic clove, peeled and quartered lengthwise
3 small zucchini, cut into slices ¼ inch thick
Flour
2 tablespoons minced parsley
½ teaspoon salt
⅛ teaspoon freshly ground white pepper
2 tablespoons (¼ stick) unsalted butter
8 eggs, lightly beaten
1 teaspoon salt
⅛ teaspoon freshly ground white pepper

Heat oil in large skillet over medium-high heat. Add garlic and sauté 1 to 2 minutes. Discard garlic. Dredge zucchini lightly in flour, shaking off excess. Add to skillet, reduce heat to medium and stir-fry until golden, about 8 to 10 minutes. Drain as much oil from skillet as possible. Sprinkle zucchini with parsley, ½ teaspoon salt and ⅛ teaspoon freshly ground white pepper. Remove from heat.

Melt butter in heavy 10-inch skillet over high heat. Quickly combine eggs with remaining salt and pepper. As soon as butter foams (it should not color), pour in egg mixture. Reduce heat to low and add zucchini, distributing evenly.

Preheat broiler.

Fry frittata slowly over direct heat, loosening edges and tilting skillet so uncooked portion runs underneath and pricking top with fork to allow uncooked portion to seep to bottom. When all but very top is softly set, slide under broiler and brown lightly, about 15 to 20 seconds. Cut into wedges and serve hot, or cool to room temperature before serving as is frequently done in Italy.

Ham and Herb Cheese Frittata

Perfect for a brunch crowd.

8 SERVINGS

¼ cup (½ stick) butter
2 onions, chopped
⅓ pound ham, cubed

12 eggs
1 cup half-and-half
1 5-ounce package chilled semisoft herb cheese, chopped
Salt and pepper

Preheat oven to 350°F. Melt butter in heavy medium skillet over medium-high heat. Add onions and cook until translucent, stirring occasionally, about 8 minutes. Add ham and sauté 2 minutes. Transfer onions and ham to 7½x12-inch glass baking dish.

Beat eggs. Whisk in half-and-half and cheese. Season with salt and pepper. Pour over onions and ham. Bake until eggs puff and center is set, about 20 minutes. Serve immediately.

Omelette D'Amour

FOR EACH SERVING:

1 3-egg omelet

FILLING

2 tablespoons chopped shallots
1 tablespoon butter
3 tablespoons chopped mushrooms
2 tablespoons dry white wine or
  vermouth
3 tablespoons chopped smoked
  oysters
2 tablespoons chopped tomato
1 tablespoon chopped parsley
¼ teaspoon lemon juice
  Salt and pepper

  Sour cream, chopped chives and
  diced tomatoes (garnish)

Sauté shallots in butter until soft. Add mushrooms and mix well. Blend in wine and cook until liquid is reduced and mixture is moist. Turn off heat.

  Mix in remaining ingredients except garnish. Place filling in center and fold in thirds. Remove to warm plate. Garnish with sour cream, chives and tomatoes.

Quick Egg-Cheese Soufflé

An easy brunch dish.

8 TO 12 SERVINGS

  Butter
25 to 30 thin slices egg bread, crusts
  removed
20 slices sharp cheddar cheese
12 eggs
 4 cups milk
  Seasoned salt

Generously butter 9x13-inch baking dish. Place layer of bread in bottom and top with half of cheese. Repeat layering. Beat eggs, milk and salt in mixing bowl until well blended. Pour mixture over bread. Cover tightly and refrigerate overnight.

  Bring soufflé to room temperature. Preheat oven to 350°F. Bake casserole until top is brown and puffy, about 45 minutes.

For variation, cooked shrimp or diced ham may be sprinkled over top of each cheese layer before adding egg.

Egg Safety

THE CARE AND HANDLING OF EGGS are the topics of a new booklet from the American Egg Board. Presented in an informative Q&A format, it covers many concerns expressed by consumers, including the use of room-temperature eggs in recipes. *The Egg Handling & Care Guide* is available by sending an S.A.S.E. (legal size) to The Incredible Edible Egg Number 33, P.O. Box 733, Park Ridge, IL 60068.

VEGETARIAN CHEESE TART

6 TO 8 SERVINGS

⅓ cup chopped cashews
1 9-inch frozen pie shell, thawed
3 tablespoons (⅜ stick) butter
3 medium zucchini, thinly sliced
2 garlic cloves, crushed
¼ teaspoon dried dill
¼ teaspoon salt
⅛ teaspoon freshly ground pepper
3 eggs, well beaten
1 cup cubed Monterey Jack cheese
2 tablespoons chopped fresh parsley

Preheat oven to 325°F. Sprinkle nuts evenly on crust. Melt butter in small skillet over medium heat. Add zucchini and garlic and sauté several minutes until softened. Sprinkle with dill, salt and pepper and toss lightly. Spoon into crust. Pour eggs over and sprinkle with cheese and parsley. Bake until tart is set, about 45 minutes.

CREAMY ZUCCHINI QUICHE

8 SERVINGS

1 9½- to 10-inch unbaked pastry shell
2 tablespoons Dijon mustard

3 cups grated zucchini
  Salt

8 large mushrooms, sliced
2 tablespoons butter

2 cups grated Monterey Jack cheese

1 cup cream cheese
½ cup whipping cream
3 egg yolks
1 whole egg
  Salt and pepper

Preheat oven to 450°F. Spread bottom of pastry with mustard and bake 10 minutes. Cool. Reduce heat to 350°F.

Place zucchini in colander, sprinkle with salt and drain about 5 minutes.

While the zucchini is draining, sauté mushrooms in butter.

Sprinkle 1 cup of the grated cheese into bottom of pastry shell. Spoon mushrooms on top. Squeeze zucchini to remove the last bit of moisture and put into pastry shell, separating and fluffing with fingers.

Beat together cream cheese, cream, egg yolks and whole egg. Season with salt and pepper. Set pastry dish on baking sheet and carefully pour in cream-egg mixture. Sprinkle remaining cheese on top. Bake 35 minutes, until top is puffed and golden and a knife inserted in center comes out clean. Let stand 5 minutes before cutting.

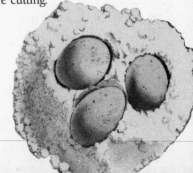

Chili Relleno Casserole

This makes a great dish for brunch or lunch.

8 SERVINGS

4 eggs
1½ cups milk
2 tablespoons all purpose flour
½ teaspoon pepper
¼ teaspoon salt
3 7-ounce cans whole green chilies, split open
4 cups shredded cheddar (about 1 pound)
4 cups shredded Monterey Jack (about 1 pound)

Lightly grease 9x13-inch glass baking dish. Beat first 5 ingredients in medium bowl to blend. Arrange chilies from 1 can in prepared dish, covering bottom completely. Sprinkle with ⅓ of each cheese. Repeat layering twice. Pour egg mixture over cheese. Let stand 30 minutes. (*Can be prepared 1 day ahead. Cover dish and refrigerate.*)

Preheat oven to 350°F. Bake until casserole is slightly puffed in center and golden brown on edges, about 45 minutes. Cool 20 minutes and serve.

MICROWAVE EGGS

To hard-cook egg, break egg into small glass measuring cup. Pierce yolk with fork. Cover cup with paper towel and cook on High until egg just begins to firm, about 40 to 50 seconds (egg will continue to cook as it stands). Immediately begin mashing with fork, blending until egg is completely hard-cooked and grated.

Crustless Spinach Quiche

6 SERVINGS

1 10-ounce package frozen chopped spinach
8 ounces Gruyère cheese, grated
2 slices day-old bread, crusts removed
6 eggs, lightly beaten
4 teaspoons grated onion
¼ teaspoon nutmeg
Salt and pepper
Sour cream (optional)

Preheat oven to 350°F. Place spinach in colander to thaw; press out all moisture. Mix spinach with cheese, bread torn into small pieces, eggs, onion, nutmeg, salt and pepper to taste. Transfer to 8-inch buttered pie plate and bake until knife inserted in center comes out clean, about 30 minutes. Serve hot or cold, with or without sour cream garnish.

Blueberry Blintzes

BLINTZES

1 cup flour
2 eggs
1 cup nonfat milk
¼ teaspoon salt

1 teaspoon butter

FILLING

1½ cups low-fat cottage cheese
1 beaten egg
2 tablespoons sugar
1 teaspoon cinnamon
¼ teaspoon salt
1 cup fresh or defrosted frozen
   blueberries
2 tablespoons breadcrumbs
   (optional)

2 teaspoons butter
   Lowfat vanilla yogurt
   Cinnamon (optional)

To make blintzes, place first 4 ingredients in blender and whirl until smooth. Refrigerate 1 hour.

To cook, melt butter in 8-inch crepe pan. Pour in just enough batter to coat bottom of pan with thin layer. Cook on both sides until faintly golden. Turn onto plate or cake rack; repeat to make remaining blintzes.

Press cottage cheese through a sieve to drain off liquid. Mix together cottage cheese, egg, sugar, cinnamon and salt. If you are using frozen berries, be sure they are completely defrosted; drain and dry thoroughly on paper towels. Gently fold ¾ cup berries into cheese. If mixture seems runny, carefully stir in breadcrumbs.

Place a spoonful of filling on each blintz, fold in ends and roll up. Melt 2 teaspoons butter in nonstick pan and sauté blintzes until golden. Serve hot with vanilla yogurt, remaining blueberries and a light dusting of cinnamon.

Cheese and Sausage Breakfast Casserole

8 white bread slices, cut into cubes
1 pound bulk pork sausage,
   crumbled and cooked
1½ cups grated sharp cheddar
10 large eggs
2 cups milk (do not use lowfat or
   nonfat)
2 teaspoons dry mustard
1 teaspoon salt
   Pepper

Grease 9x13-inch glass baking dish. Place bread in prepared dish. Top with sausage and cheese. Beat together eggs and next 3 ingredients. Season with pepper. Pour over sausage mixture. (Can be prepared 1 day ahead. Chill.)

Preheat oven to 350°F. Bake casserole until puffed and center is set, about 50 minutes. Cut into squares.

CREAMY CHEESE BLINTZES

CREPES

1 cup plus 2 tablespoons sifted all
  purpose flour
¼ cup sugar
¼ teaspoon salt
1½ cups (or more) milk
3 large eggs
2 tablespoons (¼ stick) unsalted
  butter, melted

FILLING

3 8-ounce containers cottage cheese
¾ cup sugar
1 egg
1 egg yolk
1½ teaspoons vanilla extract
1½ teaspoons orange flower water*
  (optional)

Melted butter
Powdered sugar
Sour cream

FOR CREPES: Sift first 3 ingredients into bowl. Add 1½ cups milk, eggs and 1 tablespoon butter; whisk until smooth.

Heat 6-inch-diameter crepe pan or skillet over medium-high heat. Brush lightly with some of remaining melted butter. Working quickly, ladle scant ¼ cup batter into pan, tilting so batter just coats bottom. Immediately return excess batter to bowl. Cook crepe until bottom is brown, about 2 minutes. Loosen edges with spatula. Slide crepe out onto plate and cover with waxed paper (do not cook second side). Repeat with remaining batter, stirring occasionally. (If batter becomes thick, thin with a little milk.) Adjust heat and brush pan with butter as necessary. (Crepes can be prepared 3 days ahead. Cover and refrigerate.)

FOR FILLING: Line colander with 2 layers dampened cheesecloth. Place over bowl. Transfer cheese to colander. Cover with cheesecloth, then plastic wrap. Place heavy object over cheese. Let stand 3 hours to drain.

Transfer cottage cheese to large bowl. Add ¾ cup sugar, egg, yolk, vanilla extract and orange flower water (if desired) and whisk until well blended.

Place 1 crepe cooked side up on work surface. Place 1 rounded tablespoon filling in center of crepe. Fold half of crepe over filling. Fold in sides, then roll up, enclosing filling completely. Repeat with remaining crepes and filling. (Blintzes can be prepared 1 week ahead. Cover and freeze. Thaw in refrigerator before continuing.)

Heat heavy large skillet over medium-high heat. Brush with butter. Add blintzes and cook until light brown, about 2 minutes per side. Transfer to platter. Sift powdered sugar over. Serve, passing sour cream separately.

*Available at some liquor stores and some specialty foods stores.

Sweet Potato Soufflé

Sweet potatoes are also eaten for dessert in many Latin American countries. This soufflé can be prepared several hours ahead to point of adding egg whites. Store covered at room temperature.

4 TO 6 SERVINGS

2 pounds sweet potatoes or yams

Vegetable oil

1 cup sour cream
2 tablespoons Marsala (or
   1 tablespoon honey mixed with
   1 tablespoon warm water)
¼ cup vegetable oil (preferably
   cold-pressed safflower)
1 tablespoon finely grated lemon
   peel
½ teaspoon sea salt or 1 teaspoon
   coarse salt
¼ teaspoon freshly grated nutmeg
4 egg yolks
5 egg whites

Mousseline Sauce (see following recipe)

Cook potatoes in enough boiling salted water to cover until tender, about 30 to 40 minutes (or bake in 375°F oven for 40 to 45 minutes). Let cool completely; peel. Press through strainer or food mill. Measure 2 cups purée.

Preheat oven to 400°F. Coat 1-quart soufflé dish with vegetable oil. Prepare foil collar and oil lightly; secure to dish with string or pins and set aside.

Beat purée, sour cream and Marsala in large bowl. Add ¼ cup oil, lemon peel, salt and nutmeg and mix well. Whisk in egg yolks. Beat egg whites in another large bowl until soft peaks form. Gently fold into potato mixture.

Spoon mixture into prepared dish. Place dish in oven and immediately reduce oven temperature to 375°F. Bake until soufflé is puffed and brown, about 35 minutes. Discard collar. Serve immediately. Pass sauce separately.

Mousseline Sauce

For sabayon-type sauce, omit cream.

MAKES ABOUT 1½ CUPS

3 egg yolks
1 egg
¼ cup honey
2 tablespoons Sherry, Madeira or
   Marsala or 1 teaspoon lemon,
   vanilla, orange or almond extract
⅓ cup whipping cream, whipped

Combine yolks, egg, honey and wine in top of double boiler set over gently simmering water and whisk (or use rotary beater) until mixture holds its shape. Remove from heat. Fold in whipped cream, blending well.

Spinach and Bacon Tart

6 TO 8 SERVINGS

6 slices bacon, diced
2 tablespoons (¼ stick) butter
½ cup chopped onion

1½ to 2 pounds fresh spinach,
    cooked, drained, cooled and
    squeezed dry
 3 tablespoons sour cream
1½ teaspoons dried dill weed
 2 eggs
¼ pound feta cheese, crumbled

½ pound puff pastry dough or
    4 frozen puff pastry shells
 2 tablespoons (¼ stick) butter,
    melted

Sauté bacon until crisp. Drain on paper towels. Melt 2 tablespoons butter in small skillet over medium-high heat. Add onion and sauté until golden.

Combine spinach, onion, sour cream, dill weed and eggs in processor or blender and purée. Transfer to bowl and stir in bacon and feta cheese.

Preheat oven to 300°F. Grease 8-inch round baking dish. Divide puff pastry into 4 equal parts and roll each into 8-inch round. Reserve pastry scraps. Set 1 pastry round in bottom of prepared dish. Brush with some of melted butter. Top with another pastry round. Spread spinach mixture to within 1 inch of edges on all sides. Paint pastry rim with water. Top with another pastry round, brush with butter and add final pastry layer. Press edges of pastry together. Roll out pastry scraps and cut into decorations: leaves, flowers, etc. Brush with melted butter and bake until golden, about 45 to 50 minutes.

MARMALADE SOUFFLÉ

6 SERVINGS

Butter and granulated sugar
6 egg whites
6 tablespoons powdered sugar
Finely grated peel of 1 orange
8 ounces imported orange
    marmalade
Warmed orange marmalade
(garnish)
Whipped cream and coarsely
chopped toasted almonds (garnish)

Generously butter tops of two 1½-quart double boilers. Dust heavily with granulated sugar. Beat egg whites until soft peaks form. Add powdered sugar 1 tablespoon at a time and continue beating until very stiff. Fold in orange peel. Stir about ¼ of whites into marmalade. Gently fold in remainder. Divide between double boilers and set over simmering water. Cover and cook until soufflés are set, about 70 minutes.

Carefully invert onto heated serving platter(s) and place dollop of marmalade on top of each soufflé. Serve immediately with cream and almonds.

Whipped cream can be lightly flavored with orange liqueur if desired. Platter can also be garnished with baked orange sections that have been marinated in orange liqueur.

SOUFFLE CHECKLIST

PREPARING THE SOUFFLÉ DISH For main course soufflés, butter dish and coat with a mixture of grated Parmesan cheese and breadcrumbs. Make a "collar" (long enough to encircle the dish) from a piece of waxed paper, fold it in half, and butter and crumb the upper half. Wrap the paper around the dish, making sure that the coated part extends above the rim. Fasten securely with string.

THE BASIC INGREDIENTS A standard 1½-quart soufflé consists of 1½ cups basic cream sauce, 1½ cups of the main flavor ingredient, 4 or 5 eggs, and 1 or 2 extra egg whites for added lightness.

ADDING THE EGG YOLKS When blending egg yolks with the cream sauce, first mix some of the hot sauce into the yolks, then blend into the remaining sauce. This will prevent the egg yolks from curdling.

BEATING THE EGG WHITES Egg whites should be at room temperature when beaten. Use only a grease-free stainless steel or copper bowl—no plastic. When the whites become foamy, add ⅛ teaspoon each cream of tartar and salt for every 3 egg whites.

FOLDING IN THE EGG WHITES Fold egg whites into soufflé mixture by moving a spatula downward through the center of the mixture, along the bottom of the bowl and up the side near you. Rotate the bowl a quarter turn at a time and repeat the procedure rapidly several times until blended. Do not overfold.

Do not fold in heavy main flavor ingredients, such as meat pieces. Spoon half the soufflé mixture into the dish, add the meat and cover with remaining soufflé mixture.

OVEN TEMPERATURE The oven must be preheated to 400°F; turn it down to 375°F once the soufflé is in the oven.

TESTING FOR DONENESS When the top is golden brown and 25 to 35 minutes have elapsed, test the soufflé by inserting a wire cake tester, a skewer, or a long trussing needle into the center. If any soufflé mixture clings to the tester, reduce oven temperature to 325°F and continue to bake until tester comes out clean.

THE FINAL TRICK Serve immediately.

CHEESE TIPS

BUYING

- Buy from a shop that will allow you to sample.
- Patronize a shop with a fast turnover. The cheese should be fresher.

SERVING

- Allow approximately four ounces of cheese per person at cocktail time.
- Serve cheese at room temperature in order to bring out full flavor.
- Do not remove the rind from soft, ripened cheeses. Do remove at least one side of the rind from a hard or waxed rind cheese.
- Slice a wedge from a whole cheese before serving, for a more inviting display.
- Provide each cheese with its own spreading utensil, especially soft cheeses. This is a must, particularly for all blue cheeses.
- Don't overpower delicate cheeses with strong-flavored bread, beverages or other foods.

STORING

- Store cheese in a fresh wrap after each use. Plastic wrap is best. If it does happen to develop mold, simply scrape it off; the remaining cheese is safe to use.

- Keep cheese at a consistent temperature, ideally between 50°F and 55°F. In most American refrigerators, the vegetable compartment is the best place to store cheese. It is generally warmer and retains more humidity than other sections of the refrigerator.
- Freeze cheese—if you must—in pieces no larger than one half-pound. It will freeze faster.
- Always thaw frozen cheese in the refrigerator. This helps prevent crumbling and drying.

COOKING

- Bring cheese to room temperature before use in cooking.
- Rely on the following rule for judging quantities needed: The longer the cheese is aged the more full bodied the flavor. You'll use less in cooking. With younger, milder cheeses you'll need more.
- Choose well-aged cheeses for dishes such as soufflés, which call for a light, airy texture.

CHEESE TIPS

COOKING

- Avoid stringiness in cooking by shredding, grating or breaking cheese into small cubes. This allows it to melt faster and disperse more evenly. This same effect can be achieved by blending cheese with other ingredients, such as a cream sauce, to reduce its density, or by using a double boiler or thick-bottomed pan to reduce the amount of direct heat applied for melting.

- Prevent crumbling when grating hard cheese by refrigerating until ready to use. Then remove the rind, cut into small pieces and put into a blender or food processor for a few seconds. Soft cheeses are also easier to grate when taken straight from the refrigerator.

- Remember this simple formula to measure cheese for grating: 2 ounces of bulk cheese yields ½ cup grated; 4 ounces bulk, 1 cup grated.

- Challenge yourself to improve any recipe. Put cheese between two layers of meat for hamburger patties. Put cheese into meatloaf stuffing. Add cheese to dressings for fish, fowl and salads. Melt it over vegetables. Stir it into scrambled eggs.

SAUSAGE AND TOMATO QUICHE

6 TO 8 SERVINGS

1 8-inch frozen pie crust, baked
1 cup shredded mozzarella
3 sweet Italian sausages, crumbled and cooked
2 egg yolks
1 egg
½ teaspoon salt
⅛ teaspoon dried red pepper flakes
2 cups whipping cream
1 large tomato, halved crosswise, seeded and thinly sliced
1 teaspoon dried oregano, crumbled

Preheat oven to 425°F. Place pie crust on cookie sheet. Place cheese and sausage in pie crust. Beat together yolks, egg, salt and red pepper flakes. Mix in cream. Pour into pie crust. Place tomato in circular pattern atop quiche. Sprinkle with oregano. Bake 15 minutes. Reduce oven temperature to 300°F. Bake until tester inserted in center of quiche comes out clean, about 40 minutes. Let stand 10 minutes. Serve warm.

CLASSIC OMELET

This omelet should take between 30 and 60 seconds to prepare.

1 OR 2 SERVINGS

3 large eggs
½ teaspoon salt
⅛ teaspoon freshly ground white pepper
1 teaspoon water
1 tablespoon unsalted butter
1 teaspoon unsalted butter
⅛ teaspoon freshly ground white pepper
1 teaspoon minced fresh parsley

Slowly heat a 10-inch, curved-sided, nonstick skillet over low to moderate heat (this may take as long as 10 minutes). The pan must be sufficiently hot so that a dab of butter dropped into it sizzles, but does not brown. If pan overheats, cool for a few moments and reheat slowly until it is the correct temperature. Meanwhile, combine eggs, salt, pepper and water in a small bowl and beat with whisk. When pan reaches the correct temperature, add 1 tablespoon butter and, increasing heat to medium-high, tilt pan so that melting butter coats bottom.

When butter stops foaming, add eggs all at once. Immediately begin to shake pan with one hand while simultaneously using the other hand to stir eggs in circular motion with the flat of a fork. At first, the fork should touch the bottom of the pan as you stir, so that eggs are moved all around the pan and away from the sides. As eggs begin to set, stir only the surface, always with a circular motion. When eggs are lightly set (omelet must be soft because it will continue to cook from its own interior heat after it has been removed from the pan) place filling or sauce down the center, if desired, and fold. Spread 1 teaspoon butter on top and dust with pepper and parsley.

MOZZARELLA AND TOMATO SAUCE OMELETS

6 SERVINGS

1 small onion, quartered
2 carrots, peeled, cut into 2-inch pieces
2 celery stalks, cut into 2-inch pieces
2 tablespoons olive oil
1 28-ounce can Italian plum tomatoes, drained, juices reserved, chopped
1 teaspoon dried marjoram, crumbled
1 teaspoon dried basil, crumbled
¼ teaspoon sugar
    Salt and pepper

12 eggs
6 teaspoons water
6 tablespoons butter
8 ounces mozzarella, grated

Place first 3 ingredients in processor. Chop finely using on/off turns. Heat oil in heavy large saucepan over medium heat. Add chopped vegetables and sauté until tender and beginning to brown, about 15 minutes. Add tomatoes, reserved juices, herbs and sugar. Season with salt and pepper. Cover partially and simmer until tomato sauce thickens, stirring occasionally, about 35 minutes. (*Can be prepared up to 1 month ahead. Freeze.*)

Whisk 2 eggs with 1 teaspoon water until well blended. Melt 1 tablespoon butter in nonstick skillet over medium heat. Pour egg mixture into skillet. Using spatula, lift edges of eggs as they cook, letting uncooked part run underneath until omelet is cooked but still creamy. Spoon 2 tablespoons tomato sauce over half of omelet. Sprinkle with 2 tablespoons mozzarella. Slide out onto plate, folding omelet over filling. Keep warm. Repeat process with remaining eggs, water, butter, sauce and cheese. Spoon any remaining tomato sauce over omelets.

SPINACH PUFF PASTRY QUICHE

6 SERVINGS

- ½ 17¼-ounce package (1 sheet) frozen puff pastry, thawed
- 1 3-ounce package cream cheese, room temperature
- ⅓ cup half-and-half
- 3 eggs
- 1 10-ounce package frozen chopped spinach, thawed, drained
- ½ cup grated cheddar
- ¼ cup grated Parmesan
- 2 green onions, sliced
- ¼ teaspoon salt
- ¼ teaspoon pepper

Preheat oven to 425°F. Roll puff pastry to 11-inch square. Transfer to 9-inch-diameter glass pie plate. Trim edges. Beat cream cheese in medium bowl until smooth. Gradually beat in half-and-half and eggs. Mix in remaining ingredients. Pour mixture into prepared crust. Bake until crust is golden brown and filling is set, about 25 minutes. Cool 10 minutes before serving.

Side Dishes

Without even realizing it, we often judge the success of a meal by its side dishes—the vegetables we employ to round out the main course. From Sweet Potatoes Duchesse to Stuffed Mushrooms, Broccoli Puree with Parmesan and Nutmeg to Stewed Cabbage and Apples, Green Bean Sauté to Oven-Fried Herbed Potatoes, the recipes that follow guarantee a lavish spread replete with all the trimmings.

Sweet Potatoes Duchesse

Sweet potatoes can be prepared in advance and refrigerated. Brown lightly before serving.

2 SERVINGS

2 small to medium sweet potatoes, peeled and quartered
2 tablespoons (¼ stick) butter, room temperature
1 egg yolk
⅛ teaspoon mace
⅛ teaspoon freshly grated nutmeg
Salt

Boil sweet potatoes in salted water until tender. Drain, return to pan and shake over high heat for a few seconds to evaporate any remaining moisture. Transfer to bowl and mash. Using electric mixer, beat in butter until smooth. With mixer running, add yolk and spices and whip at high speed until fluffy. Add salt to taste.

Using pastry bag fitted with open star tube, pipe potato mixture around edge of ovenproof platter. Set aside to cool. Cover loosely and refrigerate.

About 30 minutes before serving, remove platter from refrigerator and bring mixture to room temperature. Preheat broiler. Five minutes before serving, run platter under broiler until peaks and ridges of mixture are lightly browned, watching carefully.

Green Bean Sauté with Shallots

8 SERVINGS

1½ to **2** pounds green beans
2 to **3** tablespoons (¼ to ⅜ stick) butter
1 to **2** tablespoons minced shallots
Salt and freshly ground pepper

Steam or boil beans briefly until just crisp-tender. Drain well and set aside. Melt butter in large skillet over medium heat. Add shallots and sauté until golden. Add beans, salt and pepper to taste and toss lightly until heated through.

Stuffed Mushrooms

4 SERVINGS

¼ cup (½ stick) butter
3 tablespoons minced shallots
½ cup diced walnuts
8 giant mushroom caps, stems reserved and chopped
½ cup breadcrumbs
¼ teaspoon thyme
Salt and freshly ground pepper

Preheat oven to 350°F. Butter baking dish. Melt butter in medium skillet over medium-high heat. Add shallots and sauté until wilted. Add nuts and chopped mushroom stems and cook 2 minutes. Mix in breadcrumbs, thyme, and salt and pepper to taste. Fill mushroom caps, place in baking dish and bake until thoroughy heated, about 10 to 12 minutes.

CREAMED SPINACH PUREE

6 SERVINGS

¼ cup (½ stick) butter
2 10-ounce packages frozen spinach, cooked, squeezed dry and finely chopped or puréed
½ cup whipping cream
2 tablespoons grated Parmesan cheese
Pinch of grated nutmeg
Salt and freshly ground pepper

Brown butter in medium saucepan over medium heat, being careful not to burn. Mix in remaining ingredients except salt and pepper and heat through, stirring constantly. Season to taste.

SPINACH STRATEGY

FRESH

Look for bunches with crisp, flat or crinkled dark green leaves. Small leaves are preferable since larger ones are less tender. Avoid straggly, long-stemmed plants. Allow one pound of fresh spinach for two servings.

To clean, remove roots and stems, then wash leaves in a sinkful of water. Repeat washing process three times with fresh water, draining spinach between dunkings. To remove excess water, use a lettuce spinner or drain in a colander. Wrap in paper toweling, place in a plastic bag and refrigerate. Clean dry spinach should keep in the refrigerator for one week without further attention.

When preparing spinach alone, remember that little cooking time is required. Add only a small amount of water to retain nutrients. If you cook spinach immediately after cleaning, there will be enough moisture clinging to the leaves for cooking. Dry thoroughly before using in baked dishes.

FROZEN

For inclusion in a casserole, no cooking is needed beforehand, since spinach is blanched at the time of freezing. Always allow it to thaw completely in a strainer over a bowl. The liquid accumulated in the bowl can be added to soups.

When thawed, squeeze spinach dry in the corner of a towel or cheesecloth. It is imperative that this vegetable be absolutely dry when used as an ingredient in other dishes. If excess moisture remains in the vegetable, it could ooze during baking, producing a watery consistency in the entire dish.

STEAMED BABY ARTICHOKES WITH VINAIGRETTE

10 SERVINGS

6 tablespoons finely chopped
   shallots
6 tablespoons white wine vinegar
1⅓ cups safflower oil
   Salt and freshly ground pepper

1 lemon, halved
30 baby artichokes

Combine shallots and vinegar in medium bowl. Gradually whisk in oil. Season with salt and pepper. (*Can be prepared 8 hours ahead. Cover and let stand at room temperature.*)

   Fill large bowl with cold water. Squeeze in juice from lemon. Peel outer leaves from artichoke. Cut ½ inch off tip. Cut all dark green off base and stem. Place artichoke in water in bowl. Repeat with remaining artichokes. Let stand until ready to cook.

   Drain artichokes. Steam until just tender, about 20 minutes. Add to vinaigrette and toss to coat.

STEP-BY-STEP DIRECTIONS FOR PREPARING ARTICHOKES

- Lay artichoke on its side on cutting surface. Slice off stem at base to leave smooth bottom. Remove any tough or discolored bottom leaves. Cut off about an inch or so of top leaves. Using kitchen shears, trim any remaining tips from leaves. Rub base and all cut portions of artichoke with half a lemon to prevent discoloration.

- Add enough water to a large mixing bowl to cover artichokes as they are prepared. Add juice of half a lemon to make acidulated water. Using fingers, open up center of artichoke and push leaves apart. With melon scoop or sturdy teaspoon, remove and discard the fuzzy choke, scraping to clean thoroughly. As each artichoke is cleaned, drop it into acidulated water. The artichokes are now ready to be cooked.

- The choke may also be removed after artichokes have been either parboiled or fully cooked. This makes it less easy to serve them hot, but some people may find them easier to "de-fuzz" after they're cooked.

- Carbon steel knives should not be used; they will discolor artichokes and give them a metallic taste.

Broccoli Purée with Parmesan and Nutmeg

8 SERVINGS

3 pounds broccoli (about 2 large
  bunches)
6 tablespoons (¾ stick) unsalted
  butter, cut up
⅔ cup freshly grated Parmesan
  cheese
¼ teaspoon ground nutmeg

Cut broccoli stems into 1-inch pieces.
Cut tops into florets. Bring large pot of
salted water to boil. Add broccoli stems
and cook 6 minutes. Add broccoli florets
and cook until stems and florets are very
tender, about 6 more minutes. Drain well.
Set aside 10 florets. Place remaining
broccoli in processor. Add butter and
purée, stopping occasionally to scrape
down sides of bowl, about 5 minutes.
Blend in grated Parmesan cheese and
ground nutmeg. Season to taste with salt
and pepper. (*Can be prepared 1 day
ahead. Cover and refrigerate 10 florets and
broccoli purée separately. Bring florets to
room temperature before continuing.*)

Reheat broccoli purée in saucepan.
Garnish with broccoli florets and serve.

STEAMY READING

*THE COMPLETE BOOK OF STEAM
Cookery* (Jeremy P. Tarcher, 1985,
reissued 1990) by Coralie Castle
explores this healthful cooking
method, providing lots of practical
information about preparing vegetable and grain dishes. Chapters
devoted to steaming techniques,
equipment sources, plus one defin-
ing food terms and unusual ingredients, are especially helpful. The
book also offers an array of recipes
that are low in fat, salt and sugar.

Mashed Sweet Potatoes with Pecans
Citrus flavors accent a satisfying side dish.

MAKES ABOUT 9 CUPS

6 pounds yams or sweet potatoes
½ cup (1 stick) unsalted butter, cut
  into pieces, room temperature
2 tablespoons brown sugar
2 teaspoons grated lemon peel
2 teaspoons grated orange peel

2 eggs, beaten to blend
1¾ cups coarsely chopped pecans

Preheat oven to 350°F. Place yams on
baking sheet. Pierce with fork. Roast until
tender, about 1 hour 15 minutes. Cool
slightly. Peel yams. Transfer to bowl and
mash. Stir in butter, sugar, lemon peel and
orange peel. (*Can be prepared 1 day ahead.
Cover and chill.*)

Preheat oven to 350°F. Mix eggs into
yam mixture. Transfer to 3-quart baking
dish. Sprinkle pecans over. Bake until
heated through, about 1 hour.

SAUTÉED CARROTS WITH RED BELL PEPPER AND DILL

4 TO 6 SERVINGS

2 tablespoons (¼ stick) butter
1 pound carrots, peeled, thinly
  sliced
1 red bell pepper, finely chopped

¼ cup water
1 tablespoon minced fresh dill
  Salt and pepper

Melt butter in heavy large skillet over medium heat. Add carrots and sauté until crisp-tender, about 3 minutes. Add bell pepper and water. Cover and cook until vegetables are tender, 5 minutes. Add dill. Season with salt and pepper.

ASPARAGUS WITH LEMON BUTTER

A simple side dish.

10 SERVINGS

3 pounds fresh asparagus, trimmed
¼ cup fresh lemon juice
1 cup (2 sticks) unsalted butter, cut
  into 16 pieces, room temperature
  Salt and freshly ground pepper

Steam asparagus until crisp-tender, about 5 minutes. Arrange on platter.

Meanwhile, bring lemon juice to simmer in heavy medium saucepan over low heat. Gradually whisk in butter 1 piece at a time. Season with salt and pepper. Pour lemon butter sauce over asparagus. Serve immediately.

STEWED CABBAGE AND APPLES

Great with chicken, fish or pork.

12 SERVINGS

3 tablespoons butter
1 medium green cabbage head,
  finely shredded
2 large tart green apples, peeled,
  cored, thinly sliced
2 large McIntosh apples, peeled,
  cored, thinly sliced
Generous pinch of caraway seeds
  Salt and pepper
¼ cup sour cream

Melt butter in heavy large skillet over medium heat. Add cabbage, apples and caraway. Season with salt and pepper. Cook until cabbage is tender, stirring occasionally, about 8 minutes. Remove from heat and mix in sour cream. Transfer to dish and serve.

OVEN-FRIED HERBED POTATOES

This recipe doubles easily.

2 SERVINGS

2 pounds russet potatoes, cut into
  2-inch cubes
6 tablespoons olive oil
4 cloves garlic, minced
2 tablespoons minced fresh parsley
1 teaspoon dried basil, crumbled
1 teaspoon dried oregano, crumbled
  Salt and pepper

Preheat oven to 350°F. Combine potatoes, oil, garlic, herbs and pepper in large bowl and toss to coat. Spread potatoes in single layer in baking pan. Bake until brown and cooked through, turning once, about 1 hour. Season potatoes to taste with salt and serve immediately.

MASHED POTATOES WITH BRAISED TURNIPS

Potatoes are a major crop in northern New England, especially in Maine, and roots such as turnips have always played an important role in the region's cuisine.

4 SERVINGS

1 tablespoon butter
½ pound turnips, peeled, halved, cut into ¼-inch-thick slices
2 small leeks (white and light green parts only), sliced
Pepper
⅓ cup dry white wine
1 bay leaf

1 cup chicken stock or canned chicken broth
1⅓ pounds russet potatoes, peeled, cut into 2-inch pieces
¾ cup (about) milk
Salt and pepper
Chopped fresh parsley

Melt butter in heavy medium skillet over medium-high heat. Add turnips and stir to heat through. Add leeks and sauté until leeks are soft, about 5 minutes. Season with pepper. Add wine and bay leaf and boil until liquid is reduced to glaze, about 3 minutes. Add stock and boil until liquid is reduced by half, about 7 minutes. Reduce heat, cover and simmer until turnips are tender and almost no liquid remains in skillet, about 20 minutes. (*Can be made 2 hours ahead. Cover and let stand at room temperature.*)

Cook potatoes in large pot of boiling water until tender. Drain well. Purée through food mill into same pot. Reheat turnip mixture, boiling to reduce liquid

to glaze if necessary. Discard bay leaf. Purée turnip mixture through food mill into same pot with potatoes. Mix together gently, adding enough milk to thin to desired consistency. Season to taste with salt and pepper. Sprinkle with parsley and serve.

CHOLESTEROL CHECK

BEFORE HEADING OUT ON A VACATION or business trip, get the *Vest Pocket Cholesterol Counter* (Doubleday, 1990) for your travel bag. Author Susan Kagen Podell, M.S., R.D., includes fat and fiber information, dining tips, dietary guidelines and cholesterol counts for hundreds of the most common foods. It's an easy way to keep your cholesterol intake in check.

Breads

The aroma of fresh-baked bread excites even the most jaded of appetites. Some of the recipes on the following pages deliver fragrant baked goods—from Parmesan Popovers to Honey-Glazed Bran Muffins—in a matter of minutes. Others—like Braided Butter Bread, Sourdough English Muffins, and Basic Croissants—may take longer, but produce tender, golden, flavorful results as good as any bakery's.

CLASSIC FRENCH BREAD

For the best French bread, allow the dough to mature slowly. After baking, the bread can be refrigerated up to two days.

MAKES 2 LOAVES

2½ cups cool water (about 50°F)
2½ cups unbleached all purpose
    flour (10 ounces)
2½ teaspoons dry yeast

3 to 3½ cups unbleached all
    purpose flour (12 to 14 ounces)
2½ teaspoons salt

Cornmeal

Combine water, 2½ cups flour and yeast in processor and mix 30 seconds (or beat by hand 2 minutes). Transfer to large bowl. Cover with plastic wrap and let stand at room temperature for about 4 to 5 hours.

Lightly grease large bowl. Add 3 cups flour and salt to yeast mixture, blending well. Stir in enough additional flour to make soft, slightly sticky dough. Knead until dough is very elastic, adding more flour as necessary, about 15 minutes. Transfer to prepared bowl, turning to coat entire surface. Cover with plastic wrap and let rise until 2½ times original bulk, about 3 to 4 hours. Press down on dough using palm of hand. *(Dough can be prepared ahead to this point, covered and refrigerated overnight. Adjust time for second rising for chilled dough.)*

Cover dough and let rise again until 2½ times original bulk, 2½ to 3 hours.

Generously sprinkle flat baking sheet or peel with cornmeal. Press dough down using palms of hands. Turn out onto lightly floured surface. Divide dough in half. Pat each into oval. Fold each in half lengthwise, pressing edges together. Flatten slightly and fold lengthwise again. Arrange seam side down on work surface. Using sides of hands, stretch, smooth and shape dough into taut cylinder. Starting at center of each cylinder, gently stretch until each loaf is about 13 inches long. Arrange loaves on prepared baking sheet, spacing about 6 inches apart. Sprinkle lightly with flour. Cover loaves with towel and let rise at room temperature until more than doubled in volume, approximately 2 to 3 hours.

Arrange quarry tiles on center rack of oven and preheat to 450°F. Place broiler pan on lowest rack. Pour 1 cup water into broiler pan. Generously sprinkle tiles with cornmeal. Cut 4 horizontal slits in top of each loaf using razor or very sharp knife. Slide loaves from baking sheet onto hot tiles. Bake 15 minutes. Remove broiler pan from oven. Continue baking loaves until bottoms sound hollow when tapped, about 20 minutes. Cool on rack at least 1 hour before slicing.

(Loaves can be wrapped tightly and refrigerated 1 to 2 days. Reheat briefly in 400°F oven before serving.)

BASIC WHITE BREAD

For many people the words "homemade bread" conjure up just one image: golden loaves of plain white bread, crusts shining under a film of melted butter, their fragrance filling the house with warmth. Fine in texture, with a light brown crust, our Basic White Bread is perfect for sandwiches, perfect for toast; it's wonderful spread with jam, marmalade or simply with sweet butter. It is truly the basic loaf.

This recipe makes use of the rapidmix method of combining ingredients. The yeast need not be dissolved as in traditional breadbaking procedure but is instead combined with the other dry ingredients; liquid is added later. Yeast and flour can be combined ahead and stored in a cool, dry place. Rapidmix makes the mixing procedure easier and saves time, while producing loaves that rival those grandmother used to make.

BASIC WHITE BREAD

MAKES 2 LARGE LOAVES

7½ to 8 cups unbleached all purpose flour
2 envelopes dry yeast
1½ cups water, heated to 120°F to 130°F
1 cup milk, heated to 120°F to 130°F
2 tablespoons (¼ stick) butter, softened
2 tablespoons sugar
1 tablespoon salt
2 tablespoons (¼ stick) butter, melted

Lightly grease large bowl and 2 9x5-inch loaf pans; set aside.

Place 4 cups flour and yeast in large mixing bowl. Combine water, milk, softened butter, sugar and salt. Gradually beat into flour mixture, using an electric mixer or wooden spoon. When all liquid has been added, beat 2 minutes or until ingredients are well incorporated. Beat in remaining flour 1 cup at a time, until dough forms a mass and is easy to handle; it will still be sticky. (You may not need to use all the flour.)

Turn dough onto lightly floured board and knead until smooth and elastic, about 8 to 10 minutes. If using an electric mixer equipped with a dough hook, knead at medium-low speed 2 to 3 minutes. If kneading by hand, use a rhythmic push-turn-fold motion. Sprinkle additional flour on dough if it sticks excessively to hands or work surface. Break rhythm occasionally by slamming dough against board.

Form dough into a ball and place in prepared bowl,

continued on next page

BASIC WHITE BREAD

turning to coat entire surface (this will prevent a dry crust from forming). Cover with plastic wrap and a hot damp towel, and set in a warm place (80°F to 85°F) until dough has doubled in bulk, about 1¼ to 1½ hours. Punch down by pushing your fist into the center of dough, then pulling the dough edges to the center and turning dough over. Return to bowl, cover with plastic wrap and hot damp towel and allow to rise again until doubled in bulk, about 1 hour.

Knead 2 to 3 minutes to eliminate air bubbles, adding more flour if necessary to make dough easier to handle. Pinch dough with back of wooden spoon into 2 equal pieces (do not cut—cutting can break air pockets within the dough that cause bread to rise). Shape each section into a loaf by rolling into a flat oval about 9 inches long by 5 inches wide. Fold in half lengthwise, pinching seam tightly to seal. Tuck ends under and place seam side down in greased loaf pans. Cover lightly with towel and allow to rise until doubled in size, about 45 minutes.

Preheat oven to 400°F. Brush tops of loaves gently with melted butter. Place immediately on center rack of oven, leaving 2 inches between pans to permit proper heat circulation. Bake 30 minutes or until evenly browned and bottom sounds hollow when tapped. Remove loaves from pans promptly and cool on wire racks (if allowed to stand in pan, bread will become soggy).

GREAT HINTS

- To determine when dough has doubled in bulk, lightly press tips of 2 fingers into dough; if dent remains, dough has doubled. Do not use this technique to test loaves that have already been shaped.

- If using glass loaf pans, reduce oven temperature by 25°F.

- Bread baked in a shiny metal pan may require slightly longer baking time to develop a well-browned crust.

- The amount of flour required will vary each time you bake this or any bread. Flours differ in composition from one time of year to another and from one part of the country to another. Humidity can also affect the amount of flour the recipe will need.

BRAIDED BUTTER BREAD

There's nothing like homemade bread to turn a meal into a celebration. The dough requires only two minutes of kneading. You can make the pretty loaves up to a week ahead and freeze them.

MAKES 2 LOAVES

1 cup milk
½ cup (1 stick) butter, cut into pieces
½ cup sugar
½ teaspoon salt
1 envelope dry yeast
¼ cup warm water (105°F to 115°F)

1 large egg, beaten to blend, room temperature
4 cups (about) unbleached all purpose flour

1 large egg, beaten with 2 tablespoons water (glaze)

Scald milk in heavy medium saucepan. Add butter, sugar and salt. Let stand until butter melts. Pour mixture into large bowl. Cool to 105°F to 115°F. Sprinkle yeast

over ¼ cup warm water in small bowl; stir to dissolve. Let stand 10 minutes at room temperature.

Add yeast mixture and 1 beaten egg to milk mixture. Stir in enough flour, ½ cup at a time, to form soft, slightly sticky dough. Lightly grease large bowl. Add dough, turning to coat. Cover bowl with kitchen towel and let dough rise in warm, draft-free area until doubled in volume, about 2 hours.

Grease two heavy large cookie sheets. Turn dough out onto lightly floured work surface and knead until smooth, 2 minutes. Divide dough in half. Divide each half into 3 pieces. Roll each piece out between hands and floured surface to 18-inch-long rope.

Arrange 3 ropes side by side on 1 prepared sheet. Braid ropes. Pinch ends together and tuck under loaf. Repeat process with remaining 3 ropes on second cookie sheet for second loaf. Cover each loaf with kitchen towel and let rise in warm, draft-free area until almost doubled in volume, about 1 hour.

Preheat oven to 350°F. Brush egg glaze over loaves. Bake until loaves are golden brown and sound hollow when tapped on bottom, about 25 minutes. Transfer to racks and cool. *(Can be prepared 1 week ahead. Wrap tightly in foil and freeze. Thaw. Place wrapped bread on cookie sheet and rewarm in 350°F oven for about 15 minutes.)*

BASIC CROISSANTS

These layered rolls can be made over a period of several days, if desired, as there are two stopping places in the basic recipe. The croissants can also be completed in advance and frozen.

MAKES 24 CROISSANTS

2 envelopes dry yeast
¾ cup warm water (105°F to 115°F)
3¾ cups unbleached all purpose flour
½ cup milk
2 teaspoons sugar

2 teaspoons salt

2 cups (4 sticks) unsalted butter, well chilled and cut into ½-inch pieces

1 egg beaten with 1 tablespoon milk

Combine yeast and water in medium bowl and stir until yeast dissolves. Add ¾ cup flour with milk and sugar and whisk until smooth. Cover bowl with plastic wrap. Let stand in warm area, about 75°F, 1½ to 2 hours to mature. (An oven preheated to lowest setting 1 minute and then turned off works well.) About halfway through rising process, batter will bubble up, then sink down; if preparation is to be discontinued at this point, stir bubbles out of batter and refrigerate up to 24 hours; maturing process will continue.

Combine remaining 3 cups flour with salt in large bowl. Add well-chilled butter and mix, flattening butter pieces slightly between fingertips and working quickly so butter remains firm. (Refrigerate butter mixture if yeast batter is not ready to use.) Pour yeast batter into flour mixture and carefully fold in using large rubber spatula, just moistening flour without breaking up butter pieces; dough will be crumbly.

TO FOLD DOUGH: Turn dough out onto lightly floured surface. Pat dough down and roll into 18x2-inch rectangle; if dough is sticky, sprinkle top lightly with flour. Using metal spatula or pastry sheet, fold right ⅓ of dough toward center, then fold left ⅓ over to cover (as for business letter); dough will still be slightly rough. Lift folded dough off work surface, scrape surface clean and sprinkle lightly with flour. Repeat patting, rolling and folding dough 3 more times. (*If butter starts to soften and run, immediately wrap dough in plastic and freeze 10 to 15 minutes; butter pieces must remain layered throughout dough to ensure flaky pastry.*) Wrap in plastic and chill at least 45 minutes (or up to 24 hours).

TO SHAPE CROISSANTS: Pat dough into rough rectangle. Cut in half lengthwise through center, then crosswise into thirds, forming 6 equal pieces. Return 5 pieces to refrigerator. Roll remaining piece out on well-floured surface into 5½x14-inch rectrangle. Using pastry cutter or long sharp knife, divide dough in half crosswise to form two 5½x7-inch pieces. Cut each piece diagonally to form a total of 4 triangles. Using rolling pin, gently roll across shortest side of 1 triangle, until dough measures 7 inches across. Gently roll from longest side to point until dough measures 8 inches across. Holding point of triangle with one hand, loosely roll dough up from base to point with the other hand. Transfer croissants tip side down to ungreased rimmed baking sheet. Curve both ends down slightly, forming crescent. Repeat with remaining dough.

Brush croissants with egg mixture. Set aside, uncovered, in warm area (70°F to 75°F) and let rise until doubled in volume, about 1 to 2 hours; reglaze with egg mixture once during rising.

TO BAKE: Position rack in center of

oven and preheat to 450°F. Reglaze croissants with egg mixture. Bake until puffed and golden brown, about 12 to 15 minutes. Let cool on rack at least 10 minutes before serving. (*Croissants can be cooled completely, wrapped airtight and frozen. Reheat unthawed croissants in 375°F oven for 10 minutes.*)

Parmesan Popovers

6 SERVINGS

¼ cup freshly grated Parmesan cheese

1 cup milk
1 cup all purpose flour
1 tablespoon butter, melted
¼ teaspoon salt
2 large eggs

Place oven rack on next to lowest shelf. Preheat oven to 450°F. Grease 6 deep muffin or custard cups and sprinkle with Parmesan; set aside.

Combine milk, flour, butter and salt in medium bowl. Beat in eggs *just* until blended (overbeating will reduce volume). Fill cups ¾ full. Bake 15 minutes. Reduce heat to 350°F (do not open oven door) and bake 20 minutes more. Carefully remove popovers with spatula and serve.

QUICK BREADS

Add variety to your dinner roll basket with these crispy cheese triangles. All you need is pita bread, melted butter and grated Parmesan cheese. Split the pita in half horizontally with a sharp knife and brush both sides with melted butter. Sprinkle generously with Parmesan. Cut into quarters, transfer to baking sheet and toast in a 400°F oven for about 8 minutes.

Herbed biscuits spice up any company gathering and are made in minutes. Start by melting ¾ stick butter in an 8x8-inch pan and sprinkle it with an herb combination of your choice—parsley, onion flakes, dill, celery seeds—or Parmesan cheese. Top with 1 8-ounce package refrigerated biscuits and bake 12 to 15 minutes. Invert and serve immediately.

With a package of refrigerated crescent rolls and a container of cheese seasoned with garlic and herbs, such as Boursin or Rondelé, you can create wonderful mouth-watering rolls. Simply place the sheet of dough on a flat surface, spread with cheese (1 5-ounce container will fill 2 packages of rolls), then roll and bake the crescents according to package directions. Cream cheese and chopped prosciutto may be combined and used as another variation.

HERBED CHEESE BREAD

6 TO 8 SERVINGS

½ cup (1 stick) unsalted butter
1 large garlic glove, minced
1½ tablespoons fresh basil or 1½
    teaspoons dried leaves, crumbled
1 teaspoon fresh oregano or ¼
    teaspoon dried (preferably Greek)
¼ teaspoon fresh marjoram or
    generous pinch of dried
    Salt and freshly ground pepper
1 large loaf Italian or French bread,
    split in half lengthwise
3 ounces Swiss or Gruyère cheese,
    shredded
½ cup freshly grated imported
    Parmesan cheese

Combine butter, garlic, herbs, salt and pepper to taste in small saucepan and heat until butter is melted. Pour over cut sides of bread, then sprinkle with cheeses. Wrap in foil. About 20 minutes before ready to serve, place bread in oven and turn temperature to 375°F. Heat until bread is hot and crusty, about 20 minutes (if necessary, open foil to allow bread to crisp). Slice diagonally and pass in napkin-lined basket.

SWEET POTATO ROLLS

MAKES 3 DOZEN

1½ pounds sweet potatoes, peeled,
    quartered

2 envelopes fast-rising yeast
¼ cup sugar
1½ cups (3 sticks) unsalted butter,
    melted
1 cup honey
¼ cup vegetable oil
2 eggs, beaten to blend
2 teaspoons salt
3 cups all purpose flour
4 cups (about) whole wheat flour

4 cups graham cracker crumbs

Cook potatoes in large saucepan of simmering water until tender, about 20 minutes. Drain, reserving 1 cup cooking liquid. Place potatoes in medium bowl. Transfer reserved cooking liquid to large bowl; cool to 120°F to 130°F.

Sprinkle yeast and sugar over reserved warm liquid; stir to dissolve. Let yeast mixture stand until foamy, about 5 minutes. Combine potatoes, ½ cup melted butter, ½ cup honey, oil, eggs and salt in processor. Blend until smooth. Add to yeast mixture. Mix in all purpose flour. Gradually stir in enough whole wheat flour, ½ cup at a time, to form soft, slightly sticky dough. Turn dough out onto lightly floured surface and knead until smooth and elastic, adding more whole wheat flour if sticky.

Lightly oil large bowl. Add dough, turning to coat entire surface. Cover bowl with kitchen towel. Let dough rise in warm, draft-free area until doubled in volume, about 30 minutes.

Preheat oven to 400°F. Grease three 9-inch-diameter cake pans. Punch dough down. Turn dough out onto lightly floured surface and knead until smooth. Divide dough into thirds. Cut each third into

12 pieces. Roll each piece into ball. Mix remaining 1 cup melted butter and ½ cup honey until well blended. Dip each dough ball into honey mixture and then roll in graham cracker crumbs to coat. Place 12 balls in each prepared pan, arranging close together. Let stand 10 minutes. Bake until golden brown, about 25 minutes. (*Rolls can be prepared ahead. Cool completely. Wrap tightly and refrigerate 1 day or freeze up to 1 month. Reheat rolls before serving.*) Serve warm.

SOURDOUGH ENGLISH MUFFINS

MAKES 1 DOZEN MUFFINS

1 package dry yeast
½ cup lukewarm water (90°F to 105°F)
½ cup Basic Sourdough Starter (see following recipe), room temperature
⅓ cup instant nonfat dry milk
2½ teaspoons sugar
¾ teaspoon salt
¾ cup lukewarm water (90°F to 105°F)
3 to 3¾ cups all purpose flour

Cornmeal

Grease large bowl and set aside. Dissolve yeast in ½ cup lukewarm water in another large bowl and let stand 5 minutes to proof. Add starter, dry milk, sugar and salt and blend well. Mix in remaining water. Add 3 cups flour and beat until smooth. Turn dough out onto lightly floured surface and knead until smooth and elastic, adding remaining ¾ cup flour as necessary. Transfer dough to greased bowl, turning to coat all surfaces. Cover with plastic and let stand in warm, draft-free area until doubled, 1 to 1½ hours.

Sprinkle work surface and baking sheet with cornmeal. Punch dough down and turn out onto surface. Roll to thickness of about ½ inch. Cut into rounds using 3-inch cutter. Place rounds cornmeal side up on baking sheet. Cover and let stand in warm, draft-free area until almost doubled, about 1 hour.

Preheat griddle to 275°F; grease lightly. Cook muffins on both sids until lightly browned, turning once, about 10 minutes per side. Transfer to wire rack and let cool. Store in airtight plastic bags. Split and toast just before serving.

BASIC SOURDOUGH STARTER

MAKES ABOUT 1½ CUPS

1 cup lukewarm purified water (90°F to 105°F)
⅓ cup instant nonfat dry milk
3 tablespoons lowfat plain yogurt
1 cup all purpose flour

Rinse 1½- to 2-quart glass or ceramic bowl with hot water several minutes and wipe dry. Combine water and dry milk in bowl, stirring until milk is dissolved. Blend in yogurt. Cover with plastic wrap and let stand in warm draft-free area until consistency of yogurt, about 12 to 24 hours.

Using plastic spoon, gradually add flour, blending until smooth. Cover and let stand in warm draft-free area until mixture is full of bubbles and has sour aroma, about 2 to 4 days. The starter is now ready to use. Store covered in refrigerator in plastic or ceramic container (do not use glass).

SCOTTISH OAT SCONES

These are delicious served warm with butter, preserves or honey.

MAKES 12

1½ cups all purpose flour

1¼ cups old-fashioned oatmeal
¼ cup sugar
1 tablespoon baking powder
1 teaspoon cream of tartar
½ teaspoon salt
⅔ cup unsalted butter, melted
⅓ cup milk
1 egg, beaten to blend
½ cup raisins

Preheat oven to 450°F. Grease cookie sheet. Combine first 6 ingredients in large bowl. Mix together butter, milk and egg in another bowl. Add to dry ingredients and stir until just moistened. Mix in raisins. Shape dough into ball. Place on lightly floured work surface. Pat out to form ¾-inch-thick circle. Using sharp knife, cut into 12 wedges. Transfer to prepared cookie sheet. Bake until light brown, about 12 minutes. Cool slightly on rack. *(Can be prepared 1 day ahead. Cool completely. Store in airtight container.)*

BANANA NUT BREAD

MAKES 1 LOAF

¼ cup plus 1 tablespoon sour cream
1 teaspoon baking soda
½ cup (1 stick) butter, room temperature
1 cup sugar
2 eggs
1 cup mashed ripe bananas (about 2)
2 cups all purpose flour
½ teaspoon baking powder
1 cup chopped walnuts or pecans

Preheat ovn to 350°F. Grease 9x5-inch loaf pan. Combine sour cream and baking soda in small bowl. Using electric mixer, cream butter and sugar in large bowl. Beat in eggs, bananas and sour cream mixture. Sift in flour and baking powder. Stir in nuts. Spoon mixture into prepared pan. Bake until toothpick inserted into center comes out clean and loaf is golden brown, about 1 hour. Cool 10 minutes in pan. Turn loaf out onto rack and cool completely.

OLD-FASHIONED STOLLEN WITH ALMONDS

Bake some of these for the holidays, too.

MAKES 2 LOAVES

SPONGE

1⅓ cups plus 1½ teaspoons
    lukewarm milk (95°F to 100°F)
1½ teaspoons lukewarm water (95°F
    to 100°F)
1½ teaspoons sugar
1 fresh yeast cake
2⅔ cups all purpose flour

DOUGH

3⅓ cups plus 3 tablespoons (about)
    all purpose flour
1⅓ cups raisins
⅔ cup blanched slivered almonds
⅔ cup chopped candied fruit
1 cup (2 sticks) unsalted butter,
    room temperature
1 cup sugar
2 eggs
1 tablespoon ground cardamom
1 teaspoon vanilla extract
½ teaspoon salt

FOR SPONGE: Stir 1½ teaspoons lukewarm milk, 1½ teaspoons lukewarm water and 1½ teaspoons sugar in large bowl. Add yeast cake and stir until smooth. Let stand until foamy, about 10 munutes. Add flour and remaining milk and mix well. Cover and let sponge rise in warm, draft-free area until doubled in volume, about 1 hour 15 minutes.

FOR DOUGH: Mix 3 tablespoons flour with raisins, slivered almonds and candied fruit in medium bowl. Using electric mixer, beat unsalted butter and sugar in large bowl until light and fluffy. Beat in eggs, cardamom, vanilla and salt. Beat in sponge. Stir in fruit and nuts. Mix in enough remaining flour, ½ cup at a time, to form slightly sticky dough. Turn dough out onto lightly floured surface and knead until smooth and elastic, adding more flour if very sticky, about 10 minutes.

Lightly oil large bowl. Add dough, turning to coat entire surface. Cover bowl with plastic wrap. Let dough rise in warm, draft-free area until doubled in volume, about 2½ hours.

Grease heavy large cookie sheet. Punch dough down. Divide dough in half. Pat each half into 10x6-inch oval. Fold in half lengthwise; pat gently. Place on prepared sheet. Cover and let rise in warm, draft-free area until almost doubled in volume, about 2 hours.

Position rack in lowest third of oven and preheat to 350°F. Bake until loaves are golden and sound hollow when tapped on bottom, about 1 hour. Transfer to rack and cool slightly. Serve warm or at room temperature. *(Stollen can be prepared up to 1 day ahead. Cool completely. Wrap stollen in plastic and store at room temperature.)*

Sticky Cinnamon Rolls

1½ cups all purpose flour
1 cup whole wheat flour
¼ cup firmly packed brown sugar
1 envelope rapid-rise yeast
½ teaspoon salt
½ teaspoon ground cinnamon
¾ cup warm water (125°F to
   130°F)
¼ cup (½ stick) butter, melted
1 egg

1½ cups firmly packed brown sugar
1 cup (2 sticks) butter, room
   temperature
1 cup chopped walnuts
1 tablespoon ground cinnamon
½ cup raisins

Using electric mixer fitted with dough hook or paddle, mix first 6 ingredients in large bowl. Add water, butter and egg and mix until smooth dough forms, about 4 minutes. Transfer to greased bowl.

Cover with plastic and clean towel. Let rise in warm, draft-free area until doubled in volume, about 30 minutes.

Butter 9x13-inch baking dish. Bring 1 cup brown sugar and ½ cup butter to boil in heavy small saucepan. Boil 1 minute. Remove from heat and stir in ½ cup walnuts. Pour into prepared dish. Punch dough down. Roll out on lightly floured surface to 15x9-inch rectangle. Spread dough evenly with remaining ½ cup butter. Sprinkle with remaining ½ cup brown sugar and 1 tablespoon cinnamon. Sprinkle with remaining ½ cup walnuts and raisins. Roll up jellyroll style, starting at one long side. Slice dough into 1-inch-thick rounds.

Arrange dough slices cut side down in prepared dish, spacing evenly. Cover with plastic. Let rise in warm, draft-free area until doubled, about 45 minutes.

Preheat oven to 350°F. Bake rolls until golden brown, about 45 minutes. Let stand 5 minutes. Turn out onto platter. Cool slightly. Serve warm.

Honey-Glazed Bran Muffins

1 cup bran
1 cup buttermilk
1 cup all purpose flour
1 teaspoon cinnamon
1 teaspoon baking powder
½ teaspoon baking soda
½ teaspoon salt
⅓ cup (¼ stick) butter, room
   temperature
½ cup brown sugar
1 large egg
¼ cup molasses
⅓ cup raisins
⅓ cup chopped dates

GLAZE

¾ cup honey
⅓ cup corn syrup
1 tablespoon butter

Preheat oven to 400°F. Line muffin pan with 12 paper baking cups.

Combine bran and buttermilk.

Mix together flour, cinnamon, baking powder, baking soda and salt. Add all at once to bran mixture, stirring just to mix.

Cream butter, brown sugar, egg and molasses thoroughly. Blend into bran mixture. Stir in raisins and dates. Fill muffin cups ¾ full. Bake 20 to 25 minutes. Cool slightly. Remove papers.

In small saucepan combine honey, corn syrup and butter. Bring to boil over medium heat. Reduce heat and simmer 5 minutes. Place muffins, one at a time, in glaze, using a spoon to coat each one thoroughly. Place on cookie sheet until glaze is set. Serve warm with butter.

GARLIC BREAD

6 SERVINGS

½ cup (1 stick) butter, melted
4 garlic cloves, minced
1 1-pound loaf unsliced
French bread baguette, halved lengthwise
4 tablespoons grated Parmesan cheese
Paprika
Pepper

Preheat broiler. Combine butter and garlic. Place bread on baking sheet. Brush bread halves with butter mixture. Sprinkle each bread half with 2 tablespoons Parmesan. Season with paprika and pepper. Broil until golden brown. Cut into 1-inch-wide slices and serve.

ITALIAN BREAD FILLED WITH MUSHROOMS

4 TO 6 SERVINGS

1 1-pound round loaf Italian bread

2 tablespoons butter
2 tablespoons olive oil
2 small onions, chopped
2 green onions, chopped
1½ pounds mushrooms, sliced
4 ounces Gorgonzola cheese, crumbled

Preheat oven to 350°F. Using serrated knife, cut top off bread and reserve. Cut out inside of bread, leaving ¾-inch shell. Place bread and top on baking sheet. Bake until lightly toasted, about 10 minutes. Keep bread warm.

Meanwhile, melt butter with oil in heavy medium skillet over medium heat. Add both onions and sauté until golden brown, about 10 minutes. Add mushrooms and cook until tender, about 10 minutes. Reduce heat to low. Add cheese and stir until thoroughly blended, about 4 minutes (do not boil). Pour mixture into loaf. Replace top and serve, cutting base and top into wedges.

Desserts

Dessert is the crowning glory of any meal. And what could be more glorious than a classic like Three-Layer Chocolate Cake, Carrot Cake with Lemon Frosting, Crêpes Suzette, Summer Hot Fudge Sundaes, or Streusel-Topped Apple Pie? With just a little extra time spent in the kitchen, you can create a grand finale that will long remain in the memories of your friends and family.

Angel Food Cake with Chocolate Whipped Cream Icing

This luscious, fluffy icing turns homemade or purchased angel food cake into a dreamy dessert.

MAKES ABOUT 5 CUPS

1 cup powdered sugar
½ cup unsweetened cocoa powder
¼ cup milk
  Pinch of cream of tartar

2 cups chilled whipping cream
1 prepared angel food cake

Whisk powdered sugar, cocoa powder, milk and cream of tartar in large bowl until smooth. Cover and refrigerate until well chilled, about 1 hour. *(Can be prepared 4 hours ahead.)*

Using electric mixer, gradually beat cream into chocolate mixture. Continue beating until stiff peaks form. Place cake on platter. Spread top and sides of cake with icing. Slice into wedges and serve.

Carrot Cake with Lemon Frosting

8 SERVINGS

CAKE

1 pound carrots, peeled, cut into
  ½-inch pieces
1 cup corn oil
1 8-ounce can crushed
  unsweetened pineapple, drained
4 large eggs
1 tablespoon vanilla extract
3 cups unbleached all purpose
  flour
2½ cups sugar
1 tablespoon ground cinnamon
1 tablespoon baking soda
1 teaspoon salt
1½ cups coarsely chopped walnuts
  (about 6 ounces)

FROSTING

1 pound cream cheese, room
  temperature

1¼ cups (2½ sticks) unsalted butter,
  room temperature
1 tablespoon fresh lemon juice
2 teaspoons vanilla extract
5⅔ cups powdered sugar, sifted

  Fresh nonpoisonous flowers
  (such as pink roses)

FOR CAKE: Preheat oven to 350°F. Butter three 9-inch-diameter cake pans with 1½-inch-high sides. Line bottoms with waxed paper. Butter paper. Cook carrots in large pot of boiling salted water until tender, about 12 minutes. Drain. Purée in food processor, stopping occasionally to scrape down sides of bowl. Transfer to large bowl and cool.

  Whisk oil, pineapple, eggs and vanilla into carrot purée. Mix flour, sugar, cinnamon, baking soda and salt in medium bowl. Stir into purée. Mix in walnuts. Divide batter among prepared pans. Bake until tester inserted into centers comes out clean, about 35 minutes. Cool cakes in pans on racks.

FOR FROSTING: Using electric mixer, beat cream cheese, butter, lemon juice and vanilla until light and fluffy. Gradually beat in sugar. Chill until firm but spreadable, about 1 hour.

Turn cakes out of pans; peel off waxed paper. Place 1 cake on platter. Spread ¾ cup frosting over. Top with second cake. Spread ¾ cup frosting over. Top with third cake. Spread remaining frosting over top and sides of cake. (*Can be prepared 1 day ahead. Cover with cake dome and refrigerate. Let stand 3 hours at room temperature before serving.*) Garnish carrot cake with roses and serve.

SIPPING DESSERT

Sweet liqueurs like crème de menthe, crème de cacao and others like almond or coffee liqueurs make sweet endings to a spur-of-the-moment meal. Along the same line, sherry or sweet port are classic endings. Candies, macaroons or mints also add a final sweet touch.

CINNAMON-NUT CAKE
16 SERVINGS

½ cup (1 stick) butter, room temperature
1 cup firmly packed brown sugar
1 egg
1 teaspoon vanilla extract
1½ cups all purpose flour
2 teaspoons baking powder
½ teaspoon baking soda
1 cup buttermilk

½ cup plus 2 tablespoons sugar
1 teaspoon ground cinnamon
16 pecan halves

Preheat oven to 350°F. Butter and flour 9-inch square baking pan with 2-inch-high sides. Using electric mixer, cream butter with brown sugar in large bowl until fluffy. Add egg and vanilla and beat until well blended. Sift flour, baking powder and baking soda together; mix into butter alternately with buttermilk, beginning and ending with dry ingredients. Pour into prepared pan.

Mix ½ cup plus 2 tablespoons sugar and cinnamon in small bowl. Place pecan halves atop cake batter, spacing evenly. Press each nut 1 inch into batter. Spoon some sugar mixture into depressions created by pecans. Sprinkle remaining sugar over cake.

Bake cake until tester inserted into center comes out clean, about 45 minutes. Cool cake completely in pan. (*Can be prepared 1 day ahead. Cover tightly and store at room temperature.*)

CANDIED HOLIDAY FRUITCAKE

12 SERVINGS

3 cups chopped pecans (about 12 ounces)

2 cups chopped candied pineapple (about 10 ounces)

¾ cup chopped candied cherries (about 5 ounces)

⅓ cup chopped candied orange peel (about 1½ ounces)

1¾ cups plus 3 tablespoons all purpose flour

1 cup (2 sticks) butter, room temperature

1 cup sugar

5 eggs

1 tablespoon vanilla extract

1 tablespoon lemon extract

½ teaspoon baking powder

Pinch of salt

Powdered sugar

Position rack in lowest third of oven and preheat to 250°F. Grease and flour 12-cup bundt pan or tube cake pan. In large bowl, mix pecans and fruits with 3 tablespoons flour. In another large bowl, cream butter with sugar until light and fluffy. Beat in eggs 1 at a time. Stir in vanilla and lemon extracts. Sift 1¾ cups flour with baking powder and salt. Add dry ingredients to batter; stir until blended. Mix fruit mixture into batter.

Pour batter into prepared pan. Bake until golden brown and tester inserted into center comes out clean, about 2½ hours. Cool in pan on rack 15 minutes. Turn out onto rack and cool. (*Can be prepared 2 weeks ahead; wrap in foil and store at room temperature.*) Dust top of cake with powdered sugar.

Three-Layer Chocolate Cake

CAKE

1 cup milk
4 ounces unsweetened chocolate, chopped

3 cups all purpose flour
1½ teaspoons baking powder
½ teaspoon salt
¼ cup (½ stick) unsalted butter, room temperature
6 tablespoons vegetable oil
2 cups sugar
2 teaspoons vanilla extract
5 large eggs, room temperature
¼ cup grenadine syrup

FROSTING

12 ounces semisweet chocolate, chopped
1 tablespoon instant coffee granules
2 teaspoons vanilla extract
2 cups (4 sticks) unsalted butter, room temperature
2 large egg yolks
2½ cups powdered sugar

FOR CAKE: Preheat oven to 350°F. Butter three 8-inch-diameter cake pans with 2-inch-high sides. Bring milk to simmer in heavy medium saucepan. Reduce heat to low. Add chocolate and stir until melted. Cool.

Sift flour, baking powder and salt into small bowl. Using electric mixer, beat butter and oil in large bowl until well blended. Gradually beat in sugar and vanilla. Add eggs 1 at a time, beating well after each addition. Mix in dry ingredients alternately with chocolate mixture. Mix in grenadine.

Divide batter evenly among prepared pans. Bake until toothpick inserted in centers comes out clean, about 25 minutes. Cool cakes in pans on racks 10 minutes. Run small sharp knife around pan sides to loosen cake, if necessary. Turn cakes out onto racks and cool completely. (*Can be prepared 1 day ahead. Wrap cakes separately in plastic and store at room temperature.*)

FOR FROSTING: Melt chocolate in top of double boiler over simmering water, stirring until smooth. Remove from over water. Cool just to room temperature. Combine coffee granules and vanilla extract in small cup; stir to dissolve. Using electric mixer, cream butter in medium bowl until light. Add yolks 1 at a time, beating well after each addition. Add chocolate and beat well. Beat in coffee mixture. Gradually add sugar and beat until smooth.

Place 1 cake layer on plate. Spread 1 cup frosting over. Top with second cake layer. Spread 1 cup frosting over. Top with third cake layer. Spread top and sides of cake with as much remaining frosting as desired (reserve any remainder for another use). (*Can be prepared 1 day ahead. Cover with cake dome and refrigerate. Bring cake to room temperature before serving.*)

CHOCOLATE PRIMER

A guide to those chocolates frequently used in cakes and other baked or steamed desserts.

SEMISWEET CHOCOLATE is enriched with sugar and cocoa butter. It is sold in 8-ounce cakes similar to bitter chocolate or packaged as chips. (Measurements for chips are given by both package weight and by the cup.) Generally used for candy dipping, frostings, fillings, sauces and creams.

MILK CHOCOLATE is the popular ingredient used in candy bars. A combination of chocolate liquor, added cocoa butter, sugar, vanilla flavoring and milk or cream. Melted, it is used for frostings, fillings and sauces as well as in a variety of dishes such as pies, puddings and creams.

COCOA POWDER is the dry portion of the chocolate liquor that remains after most of the cocoa butter is removed. Includes various types of cocoa such as breakfast cocoa (sweetened or not), medium and low-fat cocoas and Dutch-process cocoa, which has been treated with alkali to neutralize the natural acids.

We do not advise substituting cocoa in a recipe that calls for chocolate because chocolate contains more natural cocoa butter, which gives a richer flavor. In a pinch you can substitute 3 level tablespoons of unsweetened cocoa plus 1 tablespoon butter or shortening for each ounce of chocolate. In cakes or cookies, add 1 tablespoon shortening for each 1 tablespoon of cocoa.

CHOCOLATE SYRUP is used as a flavoring and sweetener. Chocolate sauce, on the other hand, is enriched with dairy products and is used on cakes, puddings and ice creams.

WHITE CHOCOLATE is not a chocolate at all, but a preparation of vegetable fats in place of cocoa butter, with coloring and flavorings. It does not contain any chocolate liquor.

Best Chocolate Cake

24 TO 30 SERVINGS

2 cups sugar
2 cups all purpose flour
¼ cup cocoa
½ cup (1 stick) margarine or butter
1 cup water
½ cup oil
2 eggs
½ cup buttermilk
1½ teaspoons baking soda
1 teaspoon vanilla
1 16-ounce box powdered sugar
1 cup chopped nuts, toasted
¼ cup cocoa
½ cup (1 stick) margarine or butter
⅓ cup buttermilk
1 teaspoon vanilla

Preheat oven to 350°F. Combine first 3 ingredients in large bowl. Melt margarine or butter with water and oil in small saucepan over medium-high heat and bring to boil. Pour over dry ingredients and mix well. Add eggs, ½ cup buttermilk, baking soda and 1 teaspoon vanilla and blend thoroughly. Pour into 18x11-inch rectangular roasting pan. Bake until tester inserted in center of cake comes out clean, approximately 20 to 25 minutes.

Meanwhile, combine powdered sugar, nuts and remaining cocoa in mixing bowl.

Remove cake from oven. Melt remaining margarine or butter in small saucepan over medium heat. Add to sugar mixture with remaining buttermilk and vanilla and blend thoroughly. Immediately pour over cake, spreading evenly to edges. Let cake cool completely in pan.

Fudgy Brownies

MAKES 12

BROWNIES

1½ cups all purpose flour
2 teaspoons baking powder
1 teaspoon salt
1 cup (2 sticks) unsalted butter
6 ounces unsweetened chocolate, chopped
5 large eggs
2¼ cups sugar
2 teaspoons vanilla
1 cup chopped walnuts

FROSTING

½ cup (1 stick) unsalted butter
2 ounces unsweetened chocolate, chopped
¼ cup unsweetened cocoa powder
4 tablespoons milk
1 teaspoon vanilla
2 cups powdered sugar

FOR BROWNIES: Preheat oven to 350°F. Butter 9x13-inch baking pan with 2-inch-high sides. Combine first 3 ingredients in small bowl. Stir butter and chocolate in heavy small saucepan over low heat until melted and smooth. Beat eggs, sugar and vanilla in large bowl to blend. Stir in warm chocolate mixture, then dry ingredients. Mix in nuts. Pour batter into prepared pan. Bake until toothpick inserted into center comes out with moist crumbs attached, about 30 minutes. Cool.

FOR FROSTING: Stir butter and chocolate in small saucepan over low heat until melted. Stir in cocoa powder, 2 tablespoons milk and vanilla. Whisk in powdered sugar. Mix in enough remaining milk to form smooth frosting.

Frost brownies. Cut into 12 pieces. (*Can be prepared 1 day ahead. Store in airtight container.*)

Chocolate Chunk Chocolate Cookies

Mayonnaise is the surprise ingredient in these cookies.

MAKES ABOUT 48

1 18¼-ounce package chocolate fudge cake mix
10 ounces semisweet chocolate, broken into small chunks
2 5⅛-ounce packages chocolate fudge pudding mix
½ cup chopped walnuts
1½ cups mayonnaise

Preheat oven to 350°F. Combine first 4 ingredients in medium bowl. Mix in mayonnaise. Shape dough by 2 tablespoonfuls into balls. Place on ungreased cookie sheet, spacing 2 inches apart. Bake until tester inserted in centers comes out clean, about 12 minutes. Cool. (*Can be prepared 2 days ahead. Store in airtight container.*)

TOFFEE CHEESECAKE WITH CARAMEL SAUCE (COVER RECIPE)

10 SERVINGS

CRUST

1½ cups graham cracker crumbs
6 tablespoons (¾ stick) unsalted butter, melted
¼ cup firmly packed dark brown sugar

FILLING

2 pounds cream cheese, room temperature
1½ cups sugar
5 large eggs, room temperature
2½ teaspoons vanilla extract
2 teaspoons fresh lemon juice

TOPPING

1¼ cups sugar
⅓ cup water
1 cup whipping cream
½ cup (1 stick) unsalted butter, cut into small pieces, room temperature
1 teaspoon vanilla extract
¾ cup whipping cream
2 tablespoons sugar
3 1.4-ounce toffee candy bars (such as Skor), broken into pieces

FOR CRUST: Preheat oven to 350°F. Lightly butter inside of 9-inch-diameter springform pan with 2¼-inch-high sides. Combine crumbs, butter and brown sugar in small bowl. Press crumbs over bottom and 1 inch up sides of pan. Refrigerate crust.

FOR FILLING: Using electric mixer; beat cream cheese in large bowl until fluffy. Add sugar and beat until smooth. Beat in eggs 1 at a time. Mix in vanilla extract and fresh lemon juice.

Pour filling into prepared crust. Bake until cake rises about ½ inch over rim and center moves only slightly when pan is shaken, about 1 hour 15 minutes. Cool on rack. (Cake will fall as it cools, sinking in center.) Cover and refrigerate until well chilled, at least 6 hours. (Can be made 1 day ahead.)

FOR TOPPING: Heat sugar and water in heavy medium saucepan over low heat, stirring until sugar dissolves. Increase heat and boil without stirring until mixture is rich caramel color, occasionally swirling and washing down sides of pan with brush dipped into cold water, about 8 minutes. Reduce heat to very low. Add cream (mixture will bubble up) and stir until smooth. Mix in butter. Cool slightly. Mix in vanilla.

Using small sharp knife, cut around sides of pan to loosen cake. Release pan sides. Pour ⅔ cup caramel sauce into center of cake. Cover remaining caramel sauce and let stand at room temperature. Chill cake until caramel topping is almost set, about 2 hours. (Can be prepared up to 8 hours ahead.)

Whip ¾ cup cream with 2 tablespoons sugar in medium bowl until firm peaks form. Spoon cream into pastry bag fitted with star tip. Pipe cream decoratively around edge of cake. Arrange toffee pieces in whipped cream border. Refrigerate until serving.

Cut cake into wedges. Serve, passing remaining caramel sauce separately.

CHOCOLATE BREAD PUDDING

6 SERVINGS

2 cups milk
3 ounces unsweetened chocolate, chopped
3 cups fresh coarse white breadcrumbs

4 large eggs
¾ cup sugar
¼ cup (½ stick) unsalted butter, melted
1 teaspoon vanilla extract
½ teaspoon cinnamon
¼ teaspoon salt
1 cup whipping cream
¼ cup Kahlúa or other coffee liqueur

Preheat oven to 325°F. Butter 10-cup soufflé dish. Scald milk in heavy medium saucepan. Reduce heat to low. Add chocolate and stir until melted. Place breadcrumbs in large bowl; pour chocolate mixture over.

Whisk eggs, sugar, butter, vanilla, cinnamon and salt in medium bowl. Whisk in cream and Kahlúa. Pour over breadcrumb mixture and stir to combine. Transfer to prepared soufflé dish. Bake until pudding puffs up and center is almost set, about 1 hour. Serve warm.

DOUBLE LEMON CHEESSCAKE

8 SERVINGS

12 ounces cream cheese, room temperature
¾ cup sugar
2 eggs
¼ cup fresh lemon juice
1 teaspoon grated lemon peel
1 teaspoon vanilla
1 purchased 9-inch graham cracker crust

1 cup sour cream
2 tablespoons sugar
1 teaspoon vanilla

Preheat oven to 350°F. Blend first 6 ingredients in processor until smooth. Pour mixture into crust. Bake until cake filling is just set, about 35 minutes. Cool cheesecake slightly.

Combine sour cream, 2 tablespoons sugar and 1 teaspoon vanilla in small bowl. Spread mixture evenly over cheesecake. Bake 10 minutes. Cool. Refrigerate overnight. (*Can be prepared 2 days ahead.*) Cut into wedges and serve.

BUNDT CAKE

10 TO 12 SERVINGS

1 cup solid white vegetable
  shortening
2 cups sugar
2 eggs
2 teaspoons vanilla
3 cups sifted cake flour
¼ cup cocoa
2 teaspoons baking soda
2 cups milk
  Powdered sugar

Preheat oven to 350°F. Cream shortening with sugar in large bowl. Beat in eggs and vanilla until smooth. Resift flour with cocoa and baking soda into another large bowl. Repeat twice. Add flour mixture to creamed mixture alternately with milk, beating well after each addition. Pour into 12-cup bundt cake pan. Bake until tester inserted in center comes out clean, about 35 to 40 minutes. Let cool about 5 minutes. Invert onto rack and let cool completely. Dust cake lightly with powdered sugar.

CARAMEL CUSTARD

This custard is best when prepared several days ahead and refrigerated.

6 TO 8 SERVINGS

⅓ cup sugar
⅛ teaspoon cream of tartar

1 2-inch piece of vanilla bean or
  1 tablespoon vanilla
2 cups whipping cream
¼ cup sugar

5 egg yolks
1 tablespoon coffee liqueur or rum

Place 1-quart mold or eight 4-ounce custard cups in oven. Preheat oven to 325°F. Grease baking sheet.

Combine ⅓ cup sugar and cream of tartar in small, heavy-bottomed saucepan. Pour in water to cover. Cook over low heat until sugar melts, shaking pan occasionally. Increase heat and cook *without stirring* until sugar caramelizes and turns a golden mahogany brown. Quickly pour into heated mold(s) and swirl until bottom and sides of molds are evenly coated with caramel. Turn upside down on baking sheet.

Scrape seeds from vanilla beans into heavy-bottomed saucepan. Add vanilla bean, cream and remaining sugar. Cook over low heat until cream is scalded (between 180°F and 185°F).

Combine egg yolks and liqueur in mixing bowl. Whisking gently, slowly pour in scalded cream. Gently strain mixture through sieve into caramelized molds, discarding vanilla bean. Let stand several seconds, then skim off any foam.

Set molds into larger pan filled with enough warm water to come ⅔ up sides of molds. Bake 50 to 60 minutes for large mold or about 25 minutes for custard cups, until knife inserted in edge (not center) of custard comes out with a thick, curdlike coating. Remove from oven and carefully lift from water bath. Place piece of plastic wrap directly on surface of custard so a skin won't form. Cool at room temperature. Refrigerate at least 6 hours or, preferably, up to several days.

Unmold just before serving. Place mold in pan of hot water to dissolve remaining caramel and pour over custard.

SCOTCH WHISKY TRIFLE

Inspired by a trip to Scotland, where some cooks make their Christmas pudding and hard sauce with their favorite Scotch.

12 SERVINGS

COFFEE-CARAMEL CUSTARD

2⅔ cups half-and-half
 6 egg yolks
 ¾ cup firmly packed dark brown sugar
 3 tablespoons all purpose flour
1½ teaspoons vanilla extract

 1 cup plus 2 tablespoons chilled whipping cream

1¼ teaspoons instant espresso powder or instant coffee powder
 3 tablespoons Scotch whiskey

TRIFLE

 1 1-pound frozen pound cake, thawed, cut into ¾-inch cubes
 6 tablespoons Scotch whiskey
 1 cup raspberry jam (about 10½ ounces)
 2 ½-pint baskets fresh raspberries or 2 12-ounce bags frozen unsweetened raspberries, thawed
 2 large bananas, peeled, halved lengthwise, sliced

 2 cups chilled whipping cream
 3 tablespoons sugar
 3 tablespoons Scotch whiskey
 1 ½-pint basket fresh raspberries Semisweet chocolate, curled or grated

FOR CUSTARD: Scald half-and-half in heavy medium saucepan. Whisk yolks, dark brown sugar and flour in top of double boiler until smooth. Gradually whisk in hot half-and-half. Set over boiling water and stir until custard is very thick and mounds when dropped from spoon, about 6 minutes. Set top of double boiler over ice and chill custard, whisking occasionally. Mix in vanilla.

Combine 1 cup plus 2 tablespoons whipping cream and espresso powder in large bowl and stir until powder dissolves. Beat to firm peaks. Add Scotch and beat until firm. Fold cream mixture into cold custard in 2 additions. (*Can be prepared 1 day ahead. Cover and refrigerate.*)

FOR TRIFLE: Place half of pound cake cubes in 3-quart trifle bowl or glass bowl. Sprinkle with 3 tablespoons Scotch and toss. Heat jam in heavy small saucepan until just pourable. Spoon half of jam over cake and spread. Top with half of custard. Top with 1 basket or 1 package raspberries, making sure some berries show at sides of bowl. Top with half of bananas. Place remaining pound cake cubes in another bowl. Sprinkle with 3 tablespoons Scotch and toss. Layer fruit over. Spoon remaining jam over and spread. Top with remaining custard, then with 1 basket or package of raspberries and remaining banana. Cover and refrigerate until set, at least 3 hours. *(Can be prepared 1 day ahead.)*

Whip 2 cups cream and sugar in large bowl to stiff peaks. Add 3 tablespoons Scotch and beat to firm peaks. Mound cream atop trifle. Garnish with fresh raspberries and chocolate.

FROZEN LEMON MOUSSE

May be prepared up to 2 weeks in advance of serving.

12 SERVINGS

30 lemon or vanilla wafers (about)
 4 egg yolks
½ cup fresh lemon juice
¼ cup sugar
1½ tablespoons grated lemon zest
 4 egg whites
⅛ teaspoon cream of tartar
⅛ teaspoon salt

¾ cup sugar
1½ cups whipping cream

Line bottom and sides of 8- or 9-inch springform pan with wafers. Combine next 4 ingredients in large bowl and blend well. Leave at room temperature.

Beat egg whites until foamy. Add cream of tartar and salt and continue beating until soft peaks form. Gradually add remaining sugar, beating constantly until stiff and glossy. Whip cream until stiff. Gently fold whites and cream into yolk mixture. Carefully spoon into pan. Cover with foil and freeze overnight. Let mousse soften in refrigerator about 1 hour before serving.

CREPES SUZETTE

This flamboyant dessert requires good timing and a certain facility with matches. Most of the tricky work is done ahead in the privacy of the kitchen, but if you're very swift you can serve the crepes while they're still flaming.

6 SERVINGS

CREPES

(MAKES ABOUT 40; THE EXCESS CREPES CAN BE FROZEN)

1 cup flour
2 tablespoons sugar
½ teaspoon salt
3 large eggs, beaten
1 tablespoon brandy
1 teaspoon grated lemon rind
2 cups milk
2 tablespoons melted butter

Additional butter

Sift together flour, sugar and salt. Combine eggs, brandy, lemon rind and milk and add to dry ingredients. Add melted butter and mix only until ingredients are blended and consistency of light cream. Allow batter to rest for at least 30 minutes.

Heat a 6-inch crepe pan and brush bottom with butter. For each crepe, pour about 2 tablespoons of batter in pan, swirling it around until it covers the entire bottom. Cook over moderate heat 1 to 2 minutes. Turn and cook about 30 seconds. Stack crepes on plate or towel.

The crepes can be made ahead and reheated in a towel in a 350°F oven for about 10 minutes. They also can be frozen and reheated just before serving.

SAUCE

4 lumps of sugar
1 large orange, washed and dried

¼ cup (½ stick) unsalted butter
1 teaspoon lemon juice

½ cup orange liqueur

Rub sugar lumps over skin of orange so sugar will absorb orange flavor. Place sugar on board or counter and crush. Transfer to heatproof pan or inner pan of chafing dish. Add butter and lemon juice. Squeeze juice from orange into pan. Heat until butter is melted and sugar dissolved.

Warm ¼ cup liqueur *briefly*, ignite and add to sauce. Stir briskly until flames die. Add crepes (allowing 3 per serving), bathing each in sauce before folding into quarters. Warm remaining liqueur *briefly*, ignite and add to pan. Baste crepes with flaming sauce.

STREUSEL-TOPPED APPLE PIE

6 SERVINGS

5 Granny Smith apples, peeled and sliced
⅓ cup firmly packed golden brown sugar
1 tablespoon cornstarch
½ teaspoon ground cinnamon
1 frozen 9-inch deep-dish pie shell, baked

1 cup all purpose flour
½ cup sugar
½ cup (1 stick) butter, room temperature

Preheat oven to 450°F. Toss together apples, brown sugar, cornstarch and cinnamon. Place in pie crust. Mix together flour and ½ cup sugar. Add butter and cut in until mixture resembles coarse meal. Sprinkle over apples. Bake 10 minutes. Reduce oven temperature to 350°F. Bake until apples are tender, about 40 minutes. Serve pie warm.

PIE MAKER'S REMINDER LIST

A 9-inch pie requires approximately 4 cups of fruit for filling. For more flavor and better texture use instant tapioca instead of flour or cornstarch as a thickener. Bake pies in lower third of oven, but pastry shells in middle of oven.

The use of instant flour for pie dough produces a flakier crust.

To prevent soggy crusts, waterproof all pie shells with slightly beaten egg whites or apricot glaze.

Use a pastry sleeve on your rolling pin. It is washable, requires less flour for rolling, makes flakier crust.

Never overflour the board.

An excellent surface for rolling is an approximately 2-foot square of Formica-covered wood. Go to a cabinet maker. The section he cuts out of counters where the kitchen sink fits in is usually discarded. He might even give you one.

Grease all pie pans with a solid vegetable shortening before lining them with pastry.

It is better to use an electric mixer or food processor rather than fingers to mix dough. Hand heat warms the shortening. Always press dough into a flat 8-inch circle, wrap in plastic and refrigerate for 30 minutes. It chills faster than if left in a ball, and is easier to roll out.

If chilled dough is too stiff to roll, allow it to stand at room temperature until it becomes more pliable.

To prevent shrinking when baking an unfilled pie shell, prick sides and bottom of pastry with a fork; line with wax paper (not foil as it does not breathe and pastry will not brown); weigh wax paper down with enough rice or lima beans to cover bottom of the pastry.

When making a meringue, for every 3 egg whites, use ⅛ teaspoon salt, ⅛ teaspoon cream of tartar, and 6 tablespoons superfine sugar (2 tablespoons sugar per egg white). One large egg white equals 1 ounce. Superfine sugar dissolves faster than granulated.

To prevent "weeping" after a meringue is baked: when beating egg whites add sugar 1 tablespoon at a time; cover warm, not chilled, filling with meringue; meringue should be ¾ to 1 inch thick; push meringue against all sides of crust.

continued on next page

CARAMELIZED APPLE TART

Serve this homey dessert with vanilla ice cream or whipped cream.

10 SERVINGS

PASTRY

1¾ cups plus 2 tablespoons all purpose flour
1½ tablespoons sugar
½ teaspoon salt
6 tablespoons chilled solid vegetable shortening
6 tablespoons (¾ stick) chilled unsalted butter, cut into pieces
7 tablespoons (about) cold water

Nonstick vegetable oil spray

FILLING

1 cup sugar
⅓ cup fresh lemon juice
¼ cup water
1¼ teaspoons ground cinnamon
¾ teaspoon grated lemon peel
½ teaspoon ground nutmeg
⅛ teaspoon ground cloves

4 pounds tart green apples (about 10 medium)
6 tablespoons (¾ stick) unsalted butter

Vanilla ice cream or whipped cream (optional)

FOR PASTRY: Combine flour, sugar and salt in processor. Add shortening and butter and cut in using on/off turns until mixture resembles coarse meal. Using on/off turns, blend in enough water, 1 tablespoon at a time, to form dough that just holds together. Gather dough into ball; flatten into disk. Wrap in plastic and refrigerate 30 minutes. *(Can be prepared 1 day ahead. Soften dough slightly before rolling.)*

Lightly spray 10-inch-diameter tart pan with 2-inch-high sides with nonstick vegetable oil spray. Roll dough out between sheets of plastic wrap to ⅛-inch-thick round. Peel off top sheet of plastic. Invert dough into prepared pan. Press dough onto bottom and up sides of pan.

Peel off plastic. Trim edges. Chill in refrigerator 30 minutes.

Preheat oven to 375°F. Line tart crust with foil. Fill with dried beans or pie weights. Bake 15 minutes. Remove foil and beans. Pierce bottom of crust with fork. Bake crust until golden brown, about 20 minutes. Cool.

FOR FILLING: Mix first 7 ingredients in large bowl. Peel, core and quarter apples and add to sugar mixture. Let stand 45 minutes, stirring occasionally.

Preheat oven to 375°F. Melt 3 tablespoons butter in each of 2 heavy large skillets over medium-low heat. Add half of apples and their juices to each skillet and bring to simmer. Cover and cook 8 minutes. Increase heat to medium. Uncover and cook until sugar caramelizes and apples are tender, turning apples occasionally, about 12 minutes.

Arrange apples on their sides in tart crust, overlapping slightly. Spoon caramelized juices over. Bake 20 minutes. Cool slightly. (*Can be prepared 6 hours ahead.*

Let stand at room temperature.) Serve warm or at room temperature with ice cream or whipped cream.

PEANUT BUTTER AND CHOCOLATE PIE

8 SERVINGS

CRUST

1 9-inch refrigerated ready pie crust (½ 15-ounce package), room temperature

FILLING

4 large egg yolks
⅔ cup sugar
3½ tablespoons cornstarch
3 cups half-and-half
1 tablespoon unsalted butter
1 teaspoon vanilla extract
1 cup (6 ounces) semisweet chocolate chips
1 cup (6 ounces) peanut butter chips

TOPPING

1 cup chilled whipping cream
2 tablespoons powdered sugar
Grated semisweet chocolate

FOR CRUST: Preheat oven to 400°F. Transfer crust to 9-inch-diameter pie dish. Trim edges of crust and pierce all over with fork. Bake pie crust until golden brown, about 15 minutes. Cool crust completely on rack.

FOR FILLING: Place yolks in medium bowl. Combine sugar and cornstarch in heavy medium saucepan. Whisk in half-and-half. Bring mixture to boil over medium-high heat, whisking constantly. Boil 1 minute. Whisk half of mixture into yolks. Return yolk mixture to saucepan. Boil 1 minute, whisking constantly. Remove from heat. Stir in butter and vanilla. Place chocolate chips in medium bowl. Add 1 cup hot custard and stir until chocolate chips melt and mixture is smooth. Add peanut butter chips to remaining custard in saucepan and stir until peanut butter chips melt and mixture is smooth.

Spread chocolate mixture evenly into prepared crust. Gently spoon peanut butter mixture over chocolate, spreading to edge of crust. Place plastic wrap atop pie to prevent skin from forming. Cool pie on rack 1 hour. Refrigerate until set, about 2 hours. (*Can be prepared 1 day ahead.*)

FOR TOPPING: Using electric mixer, beat whipping cream in medium bowl to soft peaks. Add sugar and beat until stiff peaks form. Spoon topping into pastry bag fitted with large star tip. Pipe cream decoratively atop pie. Sprinkle with grated semisweet chocolate.

APPLE AND RAISIN CRISP

The colonists planted around 150 varieties of apples in New England, many of which can still be found today. Apples show up most often in a double-crust pie, but the crisp is also a superb showcase. Nothing more than fruit baked with a crumbly nut, flour, sugar and butter topping, it's as simple to make as it is delicious.

8 SERVINGS

TOPPING

1¼ cups old-fashioned oats
1 cup plus 2 tablespoons firmly packed brown sugar
¾ cup all purpose flour
½ teaspoon ground cinnamon
¼ teaspoon salt
¾ cup (1½ sticks) unsalted butter, room temperature
¾ cup walnuts, chopped

FILLING

4 pounds pippin or Granny Smith apples, peeled, cored, sliced
1½ cups golden or brown raisins
½ cup sugar
1 tablespoon fresh lemon juice
1 tablespoon all purpose flour
¾ teaspoon ground cinnamon

Vanilla ice cream

Preheat oven to 375°F. Butter 9x13½-inch glass baking dish.

FOR TOPPING: Mix old-fashioned oats, brown sugar, all purpose flour, ground cinnamon and salt in large bowl. Add unsalted butter and rub into mixture until coarse crumbs form. Mix in chopped walnuts.

FOR FILLING: Combine sliced apples, raisins, sugar, fresh lemon juice, flour and ground cinnamon in large bowl. Mix well to blend.

Transfer apple-raisin filling to prepared dish. Spread topping over. Bake until topping is golden brown, about 55 minutes. Serve crisp warm with scoops of vanilla ice cream.

Individual Pear and Maple Cobblers

Maple syrup is one of New England's unique gifts to the culinary world. The natural sweetener is a wonderful complement to all kinds of ingredients but is especially good when teamed with pears, which are plentiful in fall. Here they're partnered in a cobbler, an old-fashioned dessert of fruit baked with a biscuit topping. Make sure to pass whipped cream flavored with the delicate syrup.

6 SERVINGS

FILLING

3 pounds ripe Bartlett pears, peeled, quartered, cored
⅔ cup pure maple syrup
1 tablespoon plus 2 teaspoons all purpose flour
½ teaspoon vanilla extract
⅛ teaspoon (generous) ground nutmeg
1½ tablespoons butter

TOPPING

1½ cups all purpose flour
2¼ teaspoons baking powder
¼ teaspoon ground nutmeg
6 tablespoons (¾ stick) chilled unsalted butter, cut into ½-inch pieces
9 tablespoons half-and-half
9 tablespoons pure maple syrup
¾ teaspoon vanilla extract

Melted butter
Sugar
Ground nutmeg

1 cup chilled whipping cream
Additional pure maple syrup

FOR FILLING: Preheat oven to 425°F. Cut pears crosswise into ¼-inch-thick slices. Combine in large bowl with syrup, flour, vanilla extract and ground nutmeg. Divide among six ⅔-cup custard cups or soufflé dishes. Dot tops with butter. Bake until hot and bubbling, about 18 minutes.

MEANWHILE, PREPARE TOPPING: Mix first 3 ingredients in processor. Add 6 tablespoons chilled butter and cut in until mixture resembles fine meal. Transfer to large bowl. Mix half-and-half, 6 tablespoons syrup and vanilla in another bowl. Add to dry ingredients and stir until just combined.

Working quickly, drop batter in three mounds, 1 heaping tablespoon per mound, atop hot filling in each cup. Brush topping with melted butter and sprinkle with sugar and nutmeg. Immediately return cups to oven and bake 8 minutes. Reduce temperature to 375°F and bake until toppings are golden and just firm to touch, about 14 minutes. Let cool at least 15 minutes.

In medium bowl, beat 1 cup chilled cream with 3 tablespoons maple syrup to soft peaks. Serve cobbers warm with whipped cream. Drizzle additional maple syrup over.

Apple-Cranberry Crisp with Maple Whipped Cream

A hearty, down-home dessert. Accompany with a Johannisberg Riesling.

6 SERVINGS

TOPPING

1 cup rolled oats
¾ cup unbleached all purpose flour
¾ cup firmly packed dark brown sugar
1 teaspoon ground cinnamon
½ teaspoon salt
¼ teaspoon ground nutmeg
½ cup (1 stick) unsalted butter, cut into pieces
¾ cup chopped toasted walnuts

FILLING

10 large tart green apples, peeled, cored, cut into ¼-inch-thick slices
1⅓ cups cranberries
⅓ cup sugar
2 tablespoons fresh lemon juice

Maple Whipped Cream (see recipe)

FOR TOPPING: Mix first 6 ingredients in small bowl. Add butter and cut in until mixture resembles coarse meal. Mix in walnuts. *(Crumb topping can be prepared 1 day ahead. Cover and refrigerate.)*

FOR FILLING: Preheat oven to 375°F. Butter 12-cup baking dish. Combine apples, cranberries, ⅓ cup sugar and lemon juice in large bowl; toss gently.

Transfer fruit to prepared dish. Sprinkle rolled-oats topping over. Cover with foil and bake 20 minutes. Uncover and continue baking until apples are tender and topping browns, about 40 minutes. Cool slightly. Spoon crisp into bowls. Top with Maple Whipped Cream and serve.

Maple Whipped Cream

MAKES ABOUT 2 CUPS

1 cup chilled whipped cream
1 tablespoon (or more) pure maple syrup

Whip cream in large bowl to soft peaks. Beat in 1 tablespoon maple syrup. Taste, adding more maple syrup if sweeter flavor is desired. Continue whipping to firm peaks. *(Can be prepared 1 day ahead. Refrigerate.)*

PARTY PLANNING

IT'S EASY TO CHALK UP UNWANTED calories at parties and picnics. But you can prevent overindulgence by adopting a simple food-and-drink plan beforehand, suggest diet experts in *The Duke University Medical Center Book of Diet and Fitness* (Fawcett Columbine, 1990). They advise opting for low- and zero-calorie beverages, such as sparkling water or seltzer with a lime twist. Most important, once you arrive, look over what's available and decide what you will eat and how much—and stick to it.

FRESH FRUIT FINISHERS

- A tray piled with plump grapes, pears and apples provides a delightful and easy-to-prepare dessert when accompanied by one or two good cheeses. No matter what the season, there are always fresh fruits to be fashionably dressed for dessert. Serve tart plums and cracked walnuts with Camembert; pears with provolone; apricots with Brie; kumquats with a touch of Roquefort.

- Marinate 6 peeled, halved and pitted peaches in 2 tablespoons orange liqueur and ¼ cup honey. Refrigerate. When ready to serve, place 2 peach halves in each of 6 Champagne or wine glasses and add Champagne to cover. Garnish each portion with one perfect long-stemmed strawberry.

- Cut a cantaloupe in half, remove the seeds and scoop out the melon. Dice the melon and marinate in port wine for several hours. Just before serving, return the melon to the cantaloupe shell and garnish with mint.

- Put out a large crystal bowl of fresh grapefruit and orange segments and slices of pineapple dusted with finely grated coconut. Offer a small pitcher of orange liqueur.

- Mix figs in yogurt with just a skimpy sprinkling of raw or brown sugar.

- Bake bananas in their skins in a preheated 350°F oven for 20 minutes. Peel them and serve hot with a squeeze of lemon.

- Mix together ¼ cup honey and 2 tablespoons of lime juice, and spoon over thin slices of pineapple.

- Fresh fruits go well with many liqueurs. Some of our favorites are: Curaçao with oranges, pineapple or Mandarin oranges; Grand Marnier with grapefruit, oranges, tangerines or strawberries; kirsch with bananas, peaches, pineapple or melon balls and sherry with grapefruit or watermelon. And of course, Champagne with strawberries or figs in ruby port. If you must use canned fruit, try: canned pears, drained and served with Curaçao and orange juice; peaches with heavy cream and a few drops of almond extract.

- Bathe papaya and pineapple chunks in plum wine.

- With the exception of the fragile raspberry, too delicate to withstand rinsing, berries should be washed just before use.

PEARS POACHED IN RED WINE

A recipe that's a year-round delight. In summer, when peaches are in season, they can be used instead of pears to create this light and sophisticated dessert.

8 SERVINGS

3 cups dry red wine
1 cup sugar
1 cinnamon stick, broken into
   4 pieces
½ vanilla bean or 2 tablespoons
   vanilla
4 whole cloves
4 firm ripe pears, peeled

Bring red wine, sugar, cinnamon, vanilla and whole cloves to boil in heavy large saucepan. Add pears and simmer until tender but not mushy, turning occasionally, about 15 minutes. Transfer pears and syrup to large bowl. Refrigerate until well chilled, about 4 hours. (*Can be prepared 2 days ahead.*)

Cut pears lengthwise in half and remove cores. Starting ½ inch from stem end, make several lengthwise cuts in each pear half. Transfer pear halves to plates. Press gently on pears to fan slices. Serve pears with syrup.

CHOCOLATE FONDUE

12 SERVINGS

6 1-ounce squares unsweetened
   chocolate
1½ cups sugar
1 cup whipping cream
½ cup (1 stick) butter
1½ ounces (3 tablespoons) crème de
   cacao
   Cake or fruit, cut into bite-size
   pieces

Combine first 4 ingredients in double boiler over warm water and stir frequently until melted, about 10 minutes. Add crème de cacao and blend mixture well. Serve with cake or assorted fruit.

DOS AND DON'TS FOR FRUIT DIPPING

Don't attempt chocolate dipping or glazing on a hot, humid or rainy day. Fondant and frosting will work, but chocolate and glazing syrups are finicky and the dipped fruits may not harden.

Moisture is the enemy of chocolate dipping. Be sure that fruits are dry on all surfaces. Do not allow moisture of any kind to drip into the dipping medium. Do not substitute butter or margarine (they both have a moisture content) for vegetable oil in the chocolate dip.

Choose perfect fruits with no nicks or breaks in the surface which could leak moisture.

To dry very moist fruits—such as orange segments—place them in a sieve in a warm, turned-off oven for approximately 2 to 3 minutes.

Stir chocolate constantly until it is melted and well-blended with the oil. Stirring "tempers" the chocolate and ensures good color and quicker hardening after fruits have been dipped.

Keep water in the bottom of the double boiler just simmering, not boiling. If the chocolate becomes too hot, it will turn grayish and dull when hard.

Hold fruits by stems if possible; hold orange and tangerine segments by your fingertips. Drain excess coating material back into the melting pot.

Use waxed paper, aluminum foil, a cookie sheet lightly oiled or a marble slab to dry fruits on.

For perfect all-around fruits, dry by lightly spearing them on thin bamboo skewers or wooden toothpicks impaled in a block of styrofoam or on a needle flower-arranger (easily cleaned in hot water afterwards).

Do not store glazed or chocolate-coated fruits in the refrigerator. This causes the dipping material to "sweat." In the case of chocolate, the cocoa butter content causes it to turn gray and lose its sheen.

If chocolate gets too cool, it may be reheated (but never higher than 130°F) and stirred again. At 140°F it will become lumpy and grainy. Dipping glaze also may be reheated, but each time it will go darker, from clear to golden to transparent brown.

continued on next page

DOS AND DON'TS FOR FRUIT DIPPING

German sweet, semisweet and bitter chocolate are all excellent for dipping. Packaged chocolate pieces sold by various companies also are suitable and come in a wide range of flavors: mint, mocha, bitter, semisweet, milk, white, butterscotch. All may be used interchangeably for dipping fresh, dried or glazed fruit.

For glazed fruits: prepare no more than approximately two hours ahead.

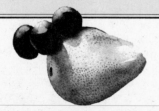

COUPE MARRON

A devastating dessert that's very simple to prepare. Ice cream can be scooped into glasses and returned to the freezer several hours before serving and garnishing.

6 SERVINGS

1½ pints vanilla ice cream, softened
  1 cup (about) imported marron (chestnut) pieces in vanilla-flavored syrup*
  ½ cup whipping cream, whipped
  3 tablespoons shaved bittersweet chocolate (optional)

Scoop ice cream into 6 wine glasses. Spoon chestnuts and their syrup over top. Garnish with whipped cream and sprinkle each serving with shaved chocolate, if desired.

    Marrons are available in jars or cans in gourmet or specialty food stores.

NEAPOLITAN SUNDAE

4 SERVINGS

  ½ cup frozen strawberries in syrup, thawed
  ½ cup sliced fresh strawberries
  4 tablespoons amaretto liqueur or brandy

  3 ounces bittersweet (not unsweetened) or semisweet chocolate, chopped
  ¼ cup plus 2 tablespoons whipping cream
  1 pint strawberry ice cream
  1 pint vanilla ice cream
  1 pint chocolate chocolate chip ice cream
  1 basket strawberries, sliced
    Whipped cream
  ½ cup sliced almonds, toasted
    Chocolate sprinkles
  4 maraschino cherries with stems, drained

Purée frozen strawberries with ½ cup

fresh strawberries in food processor. Transfer to small bowl. Stir in 1 tablespoon amaretto.

Melt chocolate with whipping cream in heavy small saucepan over low heat, stirring until mixture is smooth. Stir in remaining 3 tablespoons amaretto. Cool mixture to lukewarm.

Spoon ¼ cup chocolate sauce into each of 4 sundae dishes. Scoop some of each ice cream into each dish. Spoon some of strawberry sauce over. Top with sliced strawberries and dollop of whipped cream. Sprinkle sliced almonds and chocolate sprinkles over. Top each sundae with a maraschino cherry and serve.

ORANGE ZABAGLIONE

4 SERVINGS

6 egg yolks
2 teaspoons sugar
1 cup fresh orange juice
¼ to ½ teaspoon almond extract

Place yolks in top of double boiler. Add sugar and beat with a whisk or hand mixer until the mixture is quite thick and lemon colored. Place over hot water and add orange juice gradually, *beating constantly*. Add almond extract and continue beating until zabaglione is the consistency of thick cream. Remove from heat and spoon into tulip-shaped champagne or sherbet glasses. Serve hot or chilled.

SUMMER HOT FUDGE SUNDAES

The addition of fresh fruit gives these irresistible sundaes seasonal appeal. The rich, creamy sauce is a do-ahead.

6 TO 8 SERVINGS

FUDGE SAUCE

½ cup whipping cream
⅓ cup firmly packed brown sugar
4 ounces unsweetened chocolate (such as Baker's), chopped
½ cup orange marmalade
2 tablespoons rum

SUNDAES

1 1-pint basket strawberries, thickly sliced
2 bananas, sliced
2 peaches, peeled and sliced
2 tablespoons sugar
1 tablespoon rum
2 pints vanilla Swiss almond (such as Häagen Dazs) or chocolate chip ice cream
Toasted sliced almonds

FOR SAUCE: Stir first 4 ingredients in heavy small saucepan over low heat until melted and smooth. Add rum. Strain, pressing on solids to extract as much flavor as possible. (*Can be prepared 5 days ahead. Cover and refrigerate. Rewarm over low heat before using, stirring constantly and thinning with more cream if necessary.*)

FOR SUNDAES: Combine first 5 ingredients in medium bowl. Stir gently. Let stand for 15 to 30 minutes.

Scoop ice cream into sundae or balloon glasses. Top with warm sauce, then fruits and nuts and serve.

TERRIFIC TOPPINGS

Toast shredded coconut and slivered almonds on baking sheet in 300°F oven until light brown. Roll preshaped and frozen ice cream balls in coconut-almond mixture and place in freezer until ready to serve.

Combine 1 cup chilled dairy eggnog with ¼ cup coffee liqueur. Spoon over espresso or coffee ice cream and top with shaved chocolate.

Combine ½ cup toasted chopped walnuts, ½ cup raisins, 4 teaspoons sugar and 4 teaspoons cinnamon. Sprinkle over hot fudge sundaes.

Marinate 6 pitted dark cherries in 6 tablespoons Cognac 2 hours. Place scoop of chocolate ice cream into each of 6 frosted champagne glasses. Pour 1 jigger of cherry-chocolate liqueur over each serving and top with marinated cherry.

Pour orange liqueur over vanilla, banana or chocolate chip ice cream.

Pour equal parts crème de menthe and crème de cacao over scoop of pistachio ice cream.

Roll preshaped and frozen peach or banana ice cream balls in crushed peanut brittle until well coated.

Roll preshaped and frozen espresso, vanilla or pumpkin ice cream balls in crushed English toffee candy until well coated.

Marinate bite-size chunks of fresh pineapple in crème de menthe. Spoon over fresh coconut ice cream.

Marinate sliced strawberries, pitted cherries, raspberries, fresh peach slices or chunks of banana in cherry liqueur. Use over vanilla, coconut or lemon ice cream.

Pecan Toffee

Here's an easy recipe for toffee with a luscious, buttery flavor. It makes a terrific gift.

MAKES ABOUT 1½ POUNDS

1 cup (2 sticks) butter
1½ cups sugar
¼ teaspoon cream of tartar

6 ounces bittersweet (not unsweetened) or semisweet chocolate, finely chopped
1 cup (about 5 ounces) coarsely chopped pecans

Line 9-inch square baking pan with foil, overlapping sides. Butter foil. Melt 1 cup butter in heavy medium saucepan over medium heat. Add sugar and cream of tartar and stir until sugar dissolves. Increase heat to medium-high. Brush down sides of pan with wet pastry brush. Cook until mixture registers 310°F on candy thermometer, stirring occasionally, about 11 minutes.

Immediately pour toffee into pre-pared pan. Let stand 1 minute. Sprinkle with chocolate. Let stand 2 minutes to soften. Spread chocolate with back of spoon over toffee until melted and smooth. Sprinkle with pecans. Refrigerate until firm. Remove toffee from pan, using foil as aid. Break into 3-inch pieces. (*Can be prepared 4 days ahead. Chill in airtight container.*)

Old-Fashioned Sugar Cookies

MAKES ABOUT 2 DOZEN

2 cups all purpose flour
½ teaspoon baking powder
½ teaspoon baking soda
¼ teaspoon salt
½ cup solid vegetable shortening
¾ cup sugar
1 egg
1 teaspoon vanilla
1 teaspoon grated orange peel
3 tablespoons milk

Additional sugar

Preheat oven to 375°F. Sift flour, baking powder, baking soda and salt into medium bowl. Using electric mixer, cream shortening and sugar in large bowl. Beat in egg, vanilla and orange peel. Mix in dry ingredients alternately with milk, beginning and ending with dry ingredients.

Lightly grease 2 large cookie sheets. Roll dough out on lightly floured surface to ⅛-inch thickness. Cut 3-inch-diameter rounds using cookie or biscuit cutter. Transfer dough rounds to prepared cookie sheets. Gather and reroll scraps. Cut additional cookies. Sprinkle cookies with sugar. Bake cookies until golden brown on edges, about 14 minutes. Transfer to rack and cool completely. (*Can be prepared 1 week ahead. Store in airtight container.*)

Double Lemon Bars

MAKES 24

1½ cups all purpose flour
½ cup powdered sugar
¾ cup (1½ sticks) butter, cut into
   pieces, room temperature

4 eggs
1½ cups sugar
½ cup fresh lemon juice
1 tablespoon plus 1 teaspoon all
   purpose flour
1 tablespoon grated lemon peel

Powdered sugar

Preheat oven to 350°F. Combine 1½ cups flour and ½ cup powdered sugar in large bowl. Add butter and cut in until mixture resembles coarse meal. Press mixture into bottom of 9x13x2-inch baking dish. Bake until golden brown, about 20 minutes. Remove from oven. Maintain oven temperature.

Beat eggs, 1½ cups sugar, lemon juice, 1 tablespoon plus 1 teaspoon flour and lemon peel in medium bowl to blend. Pour into crust. Bake until mixture is set, about 20 minutes. Cool.

Cut into 24 bars. Sift powdered sugar over top before serving.

Scotch Shortbread

8 SERVINGS

1¼ cups all purpose flour
¼ cup sugar
½ cup (1 stick) butter, sliced, room
   temperature
3 tablespoons cornstarch
1 tablespoon sugar

Preheat oven to 375°F. Combine first 4 ingredients in medium bowl and blend until finely crumbled. Pat dough into 8- to 9-inch baking pan with removable bottom, spreading evenly. Press edges with tines of fork; gently prick bottom. Bake until lightly golden, about 25 minutes. Cool in pan 5 minutes. Cut into wedges using sharp knife. Sprinkle top with remaining sugar. Let cool completely in pan before serving, about 30 minutes.

Russian Tea Cakes

A version of that classic butter cookie.

MAKES ABOUT 3½ DOZEN

2¼ cups all purpose flour
¼ teaspoon salt
1 cup (2 sticks) butter, room
   temperature
½ cup powdered sugar
1 teaspoon vanilla extract
¾ cup finely chopped husked
   hazelnuts, toasted
Powdered sugar

Sift flour and salt together. Using electric mixer, cream butter in large bowl until light. Gradually add ½ cup powdered sugar and beat until fluffy. Add vanilla. Mix in dry ingredients in 3 batches. Mix in hazelnuts. Refrigerate at least 1 hour or up to 12 hours.

Preheat oven to 400°F. Form dough into 1-inch balls. Space 1 inch apart on ungreased cookie sheet. Bake until just firm to touch, about 15 minutes. Transfer to rack and cool slightly. Roll in powdered sugar. Cool completely. Roll cookies in powdered sugar again. Store in airtight container.

LEMON CRISPS

MAKES ABOUT 7 TO
8 DOZEN COOKIES

1 cup (2 sticks) unsalted butter, softened
1½ cups sugar
4 large egg yolks
Juice of 1 lemon
2 teaspoons grated lemon rind
⅜ teaspoon (¼ plus ⅛ teaspoon) lemon extract

3 cups unbleached flour
½ teaspoon salt

Cream butter and sugar until fluffy. Add yolks, lemon juice, rind and extract and continue beating until light.

Mix in flour and salt *just* until blended. Form into 2 cylinders, each 2 inches in diameter. Wrap and chill in refrigerator several hours or overnight. *Dough may also be frozen.*

Preheat oven to 375°F. Grease cookie sheets. Slice dough ⅛ inch thick and place slices 1½ inches apart on prepared sheets. Bake 8 to 10 minutes or until lightly browned around edges. Remove to rack and cool. Store tightly sealed.

Cookies will keep 1 week at room temperature or up to 3 months in freezer.

WHITE CHOCOLATE CHIP AND CASHEW COOKIES

These cookies are also great made with regular semisweet chocolate chips.

MAKES ABOUT 3 DOZEN

2½ cups all purpose flour
1 teaspoon baking soda
¼ teaspoon salt
¼ teaspoon ground nutmeg

1 cup (2 sticks) unsalted butter, room temperature
1 cup sugar
¼ cup unsulfured molasses
2 eggs
1 teaspoon vanilla
1½ cups toasted unsalted cashews (about 7½ ounces), chopped
½ cup white chocolate chips

Sift first 4 ingredients into medium bowl. Using electric mixer, cream butter, sugar and molasses in large bowl until fluffy. Beat in eggs and vanilla. Mix in dry ingredients. Add cashews and chocolate chips. Refrigerate 1 hour or overnight.

Preheat oven to 350°F. Grease cookie sheets. Drop dough by rounded tablespoonfuls onto cookie sheets, spacing 2 inches apart. Bake until golden brown, about 12 minutes. Cool on cookie sheets 2 minutes. Transfer to rack and cool completely. (*Can be prepared 1 week ahead. Store in airtight container.*)

INDEX

ACKNOWLEDGEMENTS & CREDITS

Recipes Supplied by:

Margot Alofsin
Rich Anderson
John and Dee Andronico
Yvonne Askew
Nancy Baggett
Leah M. Balk
Melanie Barnard
Ann Binder
Barbara Bishop
Charleen Borger
Jo Borinstein
Anne Boulard
Cameron Boyd
Blair Box
Daphne Bransten
Georgeanne Brennan
Debra Broeker
Mrs. William F. Buckley
James Burrows
Tracey Chrenko

Judy Collins
Shirley Corriher
Susan Countner
Russell Cronkhite
Lane S. Crowther
Anne Darby
Barbara Darnell
Terezinha de Melo
Michael De Santis
Judith Dern
Brooke Dojny
Sue Ellison
Jacqueline Fitzmaurice
Robert Gaines
Laura Gasbarro
Marcy Goldman
Rhoda Gordon
Marion Gorman
Gary and Victoria Gott

Gritti Palace, Gritti Palace
   Hotel, Venice, Italy
Donna Haje
Catherine Hilburn
Leslie Holliday
Ann Hunt
Beverly Jackson
Karen A. Kaplan
Lynne Kasper
Susan and Larry Kessler
Kristine Kidd
Elinor Klivans
Joanne and David Krajeski
Alma Lach
Jacqueline Lauby
Honey Lesser
Amy Levin
Scott Lieblich
Pat McCowan
Tom and Shari McCoy

Amanda McIntyre
Lori A. McKean
Michael McLaughlin
Mr. and Mrs. Chuck McNeil
Jinx and Jeff Morgan
Joanie Moscoe
Shirley Nielsen
Olde Port Inn, Avila Beach,
   California
Bettie Bearden Pardee
Zita Pauley
Barbara Price
Steven Raichlen
Martha Reynolds
Rebecca and Ralph Riskin
Carole Rodkey
Nell Rugee
Pamela Rupp
Kay Schlozman
Jimmie Jane Searing

Ilana Sharlin
Edena Sheldon
Lana Sills
Lani Silver
Kay Sisk
Ellen Slaby
Kristin H.R. Small
Suzanne Solberg
Marlena Spieler
Ana St. Amand
Midge Stark
R.A. Street
Dodie Thompson
Glenn Weber
Alice Welsh
Anne White
Mrs. Wadi Williams
Ernie Wolfe
Paula Zsiray

Concept:
Susan M. Allyn

Editorial development and original writing:
Norman Kolpas

Graphic design:
Sandy Douglas

Illustrations:
Michelle Burchard

Production:
Joan Valentine

Index:
Barbara Wurf

Proofreader:
Katie Goldman

Rights and permissions:
Gaylen Ducker Grody